IN THE DIRECTION OF THE PERSIAN GULF

IN THE DIRECTION
OF THE
PERSIAN GULF

The Soviet Union and the Persian Gulf

A. Aryeh Yodfat
and
M. Abir

FRANK CASS & CO. LTD.

First published 1977 in Great Britain by
FRANK CASS AND COMPANY LIMITED
Gainsborough House, Gainsborough Road
London E11 1RS, England

and in the United States of America by
FRANK CASS AND COMPANY LIMITED
c/o Biblio Distribution Center
81 Adams Drive, Totowa, New Jersey 07512

ISBN   0 7146 3071 3

Printed in Great Britain by
Robert MacLehose and Company Limited
Printers to the University of Glasgow

Contents

Maps

Abbreviations

ARAMCO	Arabian-American Oil Company
ASU	Arab Socialist Union (Egypt, Iraq)
CC	Central Committee
CENTO	Central Treaty Organization
CIA	Central Intelligence Agency (USA)
CMEA	Council for Mutual Economic Assistance (COMECON)
CP	Communist Party
CPR	Chinese People's Republic
CPSU	Communist Party of the Soviet Union
DPK	Democratic Party of Kurdistan
ELF	Eritrean Liberation Front
GDR	German Democratic Republic
GRU	Glavnoe Razvedovatel'noe Upravlenie, Main (Military) Intelligence Directorate (USSR)
ICP	Iraqi Communist Party
INOC	Iraqi National Oil Company
IPC	Iraq Petroleum Company
KGB	Komitet Gosudarstvennoy Bezopasnosti, Committee for State Security (USSR)
ME	Middle East
NATO	North Atlantic Treaty Organization
NF	National Front, see: NLF
NLF	National Liberation Front (PDRY)
OAPEC	Organization of Arab Petroleum Exporting Countries
OECD	Organization for Economic Cooperation and Development
OPEC	Organization of Petroleum Exporting Countries
PDRY	People's Democratic Republic of the Yemen
PFLO	Popular Front for the Liberation of Oman
PFLOAG	Popular Front for the Liberation of Oman and the Arabian (Persian) Gulf

PLF	Popular Liberation Front, see: PFLOAG
PRSY	People's Republic of South Yemen
RAF	Royal Air Force (Britain)
TASS	Telegraph Agency of the Soviet Union
UAE	Union of Arab Emirates
UAR	United Arab Republic (Egypt)
YAR	Yemen Arab Republic

The German Ambassador in Moscow, Count von der Schulenburg, reported that in their conversation on November 26, 1940, Molotov had said that the Soviet Government was prepared 'to accept the draft of the Four Power Pact . . . Provided that the area south of Batum and Baku in the general direction of the Persian Gulf is recognized as the centre of the aspirations of the Soviet Union'.

Documents from the Archives of the German Foreign Office

Foreword

This book attempts to analyse the Soviet Union's interest in the countries of the Persian Gulf against the background of its relations with the Arab world, and the complexities of power politics. It examines, from the nineteenth century to the present, Russia's involvement in and efforts to gain at least a foothold, if not control of this oil-rich region. The emphasis is on relatively recent and current developments, and the earlier period is covered only briefly. Particular attention is paid to the Soviet Union's interest in Persian Gulf oil, and Russian fuel resources are also discussed. Although bilateral and, to some extent, multilateral local relations are closely examined, power politics in general and in the region and the Indian Ocean are not neglected.

In addition to Soviet sources, the authors have used the Arab and Western press, periodicals and monitoring services extensively. Other sources are used to a lesser extent.

This is the first attempt to deal methodically with the subject of the USSR's interest in and efforts to reach the Persian Gulf.

In addition to the authors' collaboration, M. Abir was editorially responsible for the book as a whole.

The authors are indebted to the Leonard Davis Institute for International Relations of the Hebrew University of Jerusalem for the generous assistance provided and without whose help this study could not have been undertaken.

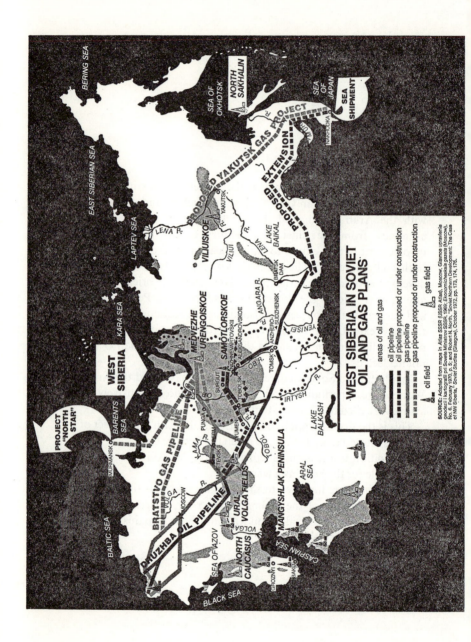

WEST SIBERIA IN SOVIET
OIL AND GAS PLANS

areas of oil and gas

oil pipeline

oil pipeline proposed or under construction

gas pipeline

gas pipeline proposed or under construction

△ oil field

△ gas field

SOURCE: Adapted from maps in Atlas SSSR (USSR Atlas), Moscow, Glavnoe upravlenie geodezii i kartografii pri Sovete Ministrov SSSR, 1969; Ekonomicheskaia gazeta (Moscow), No. 6, February 1970, p. 5; and Robert N. North, "Soviet Northern Development: The Case of NW Siberia," Soviet Studies (Glasgow), October 1972, pp. 173, 174, 176.

CHAPTER I

Oil: The USSR and the Persian Gulf

Until World War I, Tsarist Russia was believed to have the largest oil reserves in the Eastern hemisphere. For years its production was greater than any other country except the United States, and in certain years surpassed even the American total. Baku, a seaport in the area where the Russian oil industry developed, came under Russian control in the early nineteenth century. The first refinery for the production of illuminating oil was established near there in 1859.[1] Actual oil exploitation began in about 1870, when foreign investors, the Nobel brothers and later the Rothschilds, began to develop the Baku region and other nearby oil fields. As the demand for oil grew, other European countries became interested in the Russian source because it was close to central and western European centres of consumption, its wells were shallow and very productive and transportation through the Black Sea was relatively easy. From a maximum of 42,000 tons annually before 1870, Russian oil production rose to a peak of 11,500,000 tons in 1901, a year in which Russia produced over half the world supply and exported more than 1,000,000 tons. In subsequent years there was a distinct decline in Russian production, while that from other countries, particularly the United States, increased.[2]

Oil was discovered in the southwestern part of Persia in 1908, the year after the signing of the Anglo-Russian Agreement. It is doubtful if Britain would have consented to the terms of the Agreement if oil had been discovered earlier, because the 1907 treaty classified the oil-rich area and, in fact, the greater part of the Gulf littoral, as a neutral zone. The Persian Gulf, which Britain regarded as India's line of defence, had been only second in importance to the Suez Canal as a transportation route until then. After the discovery of oil in the area, it became important in its own right, and together with the oil fields on the shores of the Gulf, required defence and protection. Even before World War I, the British had shifted from coal to oil as an energy source, and the importance of the Gulf during the War rose accordingly. British military operations in Mesopotamia were, to a considerable extent, directed toward protecting Persian oil fields.

Oil was also an important factor in the Turkish–German military campaigns in the Caucasus during the first years of World War I and in the British campaigns in that area after the November 1917 Bolshevik rise to power. Each nation had as its goal control of the oil fields at Baku.[3]

Soviet forces entered Baku in April 1920. Its oil fields were nationalized, gradually reconstructed and developed as a Soviet state trust to become the main source of Soviet oil.

Crude Oil Production[4]
(thousand metric tons)

	Russia/USSR	*World Total*
1916	9,058	63,000
1917	8,680	69,200
1921	3,987	105,500
1926	8,878	151,000
1931	22,814	188,900
1936	26,699	246,600
1941	33,364	305,600
1946	21,746	375,100
1951	42,253	587,100
1956	83,806	837,500
1961	166,068	1,119,400
1966	267,800	1,641,300

There was a marked decline in Russian oil production in 1917, the year of the Revolution, a much greater decline during the civil war, and only in 1926 did production approach the pre-Revolutionary level. Much oil was exported, as it was the largest single source of foreign exchange; about 20 per cent of all exports by value.[5] Local Soviet use of oil was still limited. Motor transport had not been developed and industry and railways used mainly coal and, later, hydro-electric, power. As the Soviets had neither the equipment, capital, nor the skilled manpower to develop and expand oil production, or to construct pipelines and refineries, they were ready to grant concessions to foreign companies.[6]

Western oil companies first tried to end the Soviet regime and regain their nationalized oil fields and concessions. When the regime began to look strong and unlikely to be replaced, attempts were made by the companies to have concessions awarded to them. When that also failed, they tried at least to purchase large quantities of Soviet oil. The success or failure of such attempts determined their attitudes and, to a great extent, those of their respective governments to the USSR and the Soviet regime, to the decisions to cooperate or boycott, to be friendly or hostile. As one observer described the situation in 1926:

> Russia's petroleum wealth was for years a liability to Soviet diplomacy. Moscow's relations to Washington would long ago have been more friendly than they are today, had there been no petroleum resources at Baku to which the Standard Oil laid claim. . . . The Anglo-Soviet Treaty of 1924 might never have been scrapped had not Royal Dutch-Shell inspired the British creditors to oppose the agreement because it might have prejudiced Shell's possibility of regaining title to its former holdings in the Caucasus.[7]

The trauma of relations with Western oil companies and their activities against the USSR and the Soviet regime long remained in the minds of Soviet leaders. Those companies were seen as a powerful enemy, manipulating governments behind the scenes and impeding any improvement in relations between the USSR and Western countries, even after the oil companies' influence on their governments had decreased.

World War II demonstrated as never before, the importance of oil for military use and for future economic development. The USSR was fortunate that, just when the Caucasus oil fields were drying up, rich new deposits were discovered between the Volga and the Ural Mountains, which the Soviets called the 'Second Baku'. By 1952, the 'Second Baku' supplied about 40 per cent of Soviet oil production;[8] by 1960 – 73 per cent, while the Caucasus fields produced only about 17 per cent of the total output.[9] Clearly, the centre of Soviet oil production was shifting from the Caucasus toward the north and east. At the same time, the importance of the Russian share of oil production in the Middle East and the Persian Gulf in particular increased.

In the mid-1950s, when the world oil market was saturated, the USSR increased its oil exports to Western countries. Oil was clearly becoming, in Soviet eyes, a political tool as well as a commodity. The motivation for this policy was not merely the traditional need to earn foreign currency, but also the desire to undermine the boycott on Soviet products which was a partial outcome of the 'Cold War'. The

Soviets not only sold their oil at bargain prices but were ready to barter oil against manufactured goods and agricultural products, such as Egyptian cotton or Israeli oranges.[10]

Soviet oil was sold without regard to economic factors and, ironically, the Arab oil-producing countries were the first to suffer from this policy. Thus, a common interest arose between the major Western oil companies (who warned their governments and the world of the danger of dependency on Soviet oil) and the major oil-producing countries.

It is of course difficult to prove that the Soviet Union intended to deny the West the cheaper and higher-quality Gulf oil. It is obvious that the 1956 Suez war, the closure of the Suez Canal and the impact of the oil shortage on Europe were in themselves sufficient to convince the Soviet leadership of the crucial importance of Gulf oil to the Western world and of Egypt's importance to future Soviet plans. Egypt's President, Jamal 'Abd an-Nasser, pursued policies which suited Soviet aims. They saw his nationalizations, at a future date, of other resources, including oil.

When Egypt closed the Suez Canal and Syria halted the flow of oil through the Iraq Petroleum Company (IPC) pipeline where it passed through Syrian territory, Western European countries suffered temporary shortages. In the context of the 1950s, however, Europe's problems emanated not from a shortage of oil supplies, but rather, from a means of transporting it. It was not long before Europe's oil needs were supplied from other sources.

Thus, conflicting interests developed in the Arab world between oil-producing countries, which feared a loss of revenue, and the anti-Israel 'confrontation states', which were non-oil producers, more extreme and ready to cooperate with the Soviet Union. It was quite natural that the conservative Persian Gulf oil producers began to fear increasing Soviet attempts to use Egypt to undermine their regimes. Iraq may serve as an example of such differing interests. Even under the radical regime which came into power following the July 1958 revolution Iraq continued to sell oil to its traditional customers.

The United States, recognizing the negative result of its own role in the 1956–57 Suez conflict, joined with its Western allies in developing a more active policy to stop Soviet penetration into the region. One of the manifestations of this policy was the 'Eisenhower Doctrine', which was directed, although not exclusively, toward the Persian Gulf. The possibility was only slight that the Soviets would try to control the area by force; it was far more likely that they would gradually build up their influence there through Egypt and other pro-Soviet 'progressive' Arab states.

Many traditional dependable Soviet oil fields have already reached their peak capacity and are beginning to dry up. New explorations in the northern Caucasus and in the Volga–Ural region (the major source of Soviet oil production) have been disappointing. Oil fields, hitherto considered too expensive to operate, have been re-opened. However, opening new fields in more distant areas demands enormous capital investment which is still unavailable, as well as skilled manpower which is also in short supply. Despite a proliferation of institutes of higher learning, there are still too few oil geologists, oil economists, managers, and other specialists. There are simply not enough suitable candidates for the majority of positions in the petroleum industry. The shift of oil production centres to remote and difficult areas also diminishes the amount of time workers are willing to remain on the job, despite relatively generous financial compensation. In turn this tendency increases the necessity for greater automation of operation, the equipment and investment capital for which have to be imported from Western countries.

Especially rich, high-grade oil fields, almost totally without sulphur, were discovered in the Ob river basin, in the Tyumen area of western Siberia. Production there rose from zero in the mid-1960s to 30 million tons in 1970, 56 million tons in 1972, with targets of 100–120 million tons for 1975 and 230–260 million tons in 1980 (which will amount to 40 per cent of the country's planned production). Increased production is also expected in other distant and somewhat inaccessible areas such as western Kazakhstan and eastern Siberia. The entire Soviet production of oil was 353 million tons in 1970, 394 million in 1972, 430 million in 1973. The 1971–75 Five Year Plan includes production of 480–500 million tons in 1975, and 600–630 million tons are planned for 1980.[11]

It is very difficult to predict whether the above targets will be met. Plans can fail, in which case the USSR might require foreign oil. The Tyumen fields, which are expected to supply the greater portion of Soviet oil, are located at 60° north latitude. This is an area of strong frosts and permafrost ground, in which drilling and pipe-laying are very difficult. In summer, the upper crust turns into swamp

B

which breeds mosquitoes and renders the movement of equipment almost impossible. Access to this area is still limited and few people are attracted to an area which lacks an infrastructure of electrical power, transportation and is so far from the main consumption centres.[12] When oil is discovered where there is a minimal resident population, conditions must be improved in order to attract additional manpower to the area. Building houses, shops, restaurants and other facilities adds to the cost, thereby raising the price of Soviet oil. Moreover, the Soviets no longer 'play with prices', exporting oil at bargain prices as they did when production was almost entirely in roubles. Because of today's more expensive technology and equipment (at least in part imported) and higher production costs, they can no longer afford cheap exports and therefore have an interest in a rise in oil prices.

Also, Soviet consumption has risen as a result of the expansion of the economy, industry (particularly chemicals), technology and military power; the change from the use of coal to oil as a fuel supply for rail traffic (which turned to diesel fuel only in the 1960s), airlines and shipping; as well as from an increase in the number of motor vehicles. The USSR has not yet entered the era of private automobiles; when it does, consumption will increase still more, leaving less oil for export and creating a need for organized gasoline marketing and distribution, which does not yet exist. This rise in oil consumption will occur even with the development of new alternative energy sources, such as nuclear power.[13]

Oil development requires enormous investments. But so do defence, agriculture, electrification, heavy industry and consumer goods – all of them competing for the same limited resources. This makes the need for foreign assistance in the development of the oil industry still more imperative.

This situation makes it probable that in the near future the USSR may no longer be able to maintain its self-sufficiency. The question was first posed by a Polish journalist, Stanislaw Albinowski, writing on foreign trade in the Polish weekly *Polityka*, September 24, 1966. After analysing supply and consumption of oil in the USSR, he came to the conclusion that by 1980, the USSR will not only be unable to export oil, but will have to import 90 million tons for itself and its allies.

Boris Rachkov, a Soviet journalist who specializes in oil affairs, wrote in May 1969, that the USSR and its allies would need to import about 100 million tons of oil annually by 1980. The statement came in rebuttal to those who were arguing that the USSR was a competitor of the Middle Eastern oil-producing countries. Soviet fuel consumption, Rachkov said, was growing rapidly and it had already begun to import Arab and Iranian oil. Soviet oil exports had reached their peak, but the USSR sold to the West less than 50 million tons of oil products.[14]

USSR oil (million tons)[15]

Year	Production	Exports	Consumption
1968	295.2	86.2	209.0
1969	313.5	90.8	222.7
1970	336.4	95.8	240.6
1971	356.8	105.1	251.7
1972	377.7	107.0	270.7
1973	429.0	113.5	315.5
1975*	473.7	135.0	338.7
1980*	611.0	111.0	500.0

*Estimates

According to the above estimates, in 1980 Soviet exports will be near the present level. According to OECD estimates, by 1980 Soviet domestic needs will be much greater, 613 million tons, and production of 616 million tons will leave almost nothing for export.[16]

In 1973, sales of Soviet oil amounted to 50.5 million tons to the non-communist world and 63 million to the communist world.[17] Such exports reaped many advantages for the USSR. Sales to Western Europe and Japan, even when the USSR serves only as a middleman for oil from another source, provide the USSR with much-needed hard currency and are the country's biggest single source of foreign exchange ($570 million in 1972).[18] They influence political relations between buyer and seller by promoting purchases of Soviet products. When, for a short time after the June 1967 Arab–Israeli war, the Arab states refused to sell oil to certain Western powers, the USSR used that opportunity to increase its oil exports and to appear as a reliable oil supplier.

The dramatic rise in oil prices in 1973 was undoubtedly advantageous to the Soviet Union. It probably solved some of the more pressing problems the USSR faced when trying to begin production in western Siberia and attempting to attract Western and Japanese capital and technology for that purpose. Moreover, it had a most beneficial impact on Soviet foreign currency earning and opened new horizons for the Soviet economy and politics.

The USSR's Eastern European allies, with the exception of Rumania, are all dependent on Soviet oil. The USSR is committed to supplying their needs as well as those of North Vietnam and Cuba.[19] In some of these countries, consumption is growing at a much greater rate than in the USSR; the changeover from solid fuels, mainly coal, to liquid fuel was made in Western countries many years ago; a high proportion of Eastern Europe's energy is still derived from coal. In 1971 these countries needed about 48–50 million tons of oil and will need about 80–100 million tons in 1980.[20] Supplying oil to those countries does not, of course, provide the USSR with any hard currency, and the equipment given in exchange is less advanced than that received from Western countries; but it does give the USSR extensive control over their economies. The question is whether the USSR will be able to supply their growing needs for oil in the future. In the mid-1960s the USSR informed COMECON members that by the 1970s it would no longer be able to fulfil their oil requirements and advised them to look for additional sources. Nevertheless, Russia preferred to supply them with oil as long as it were possible.

The USSR has great reserves of natural gas that are much less extensively exploited than its oil.[21] Most of them are in distant areas, difficult and expensive to develop; more than half located in Western Siberia. In the USSR there is an enormous network of oil and gas pipelines with pumping and compressor stations, and there are plans to expand the system. Scheduled production is 300,000–320,000 million cubic metres of gas in 1975.[22]

To overcome enormous pipeline shortages, the USSR imports substantial quantities from West Germany. Many more are needed. They may come from the United States which has rich experience in the relevant pipeline technology. The Soviets are interested in building oil and gas pipelines from West and East Siberia to the port of Nakhodka, east of Vladivostok, for which negotiations are being conducted between the Soviets and the Japanese. A gas line is planned from West Siberia to Murmansk and Soviet–American talks are under way concerning American investment in Soviet development in exchange for exports of Soviet gas to the United States.

The problems with which Soviet planners are faced involve present oil shortages, methods of avoiding shortages, whether to increase oil production themselves or with foreign assistance. At present, there are four alternatives:

(a) Decreasing internal Soviet consumption. This would not be easy to implement because it would restrict the economic development of the country.

(b) Enabling Soviet allies to buy crude oil by themselves. It would give those countries a greater measure of economic independence than the Soviets wish and perhaps a greater measure of political autonomy. The Soviets would prefer to avoid, or at least to delay such a change; eventually they will have no choice but to permit it. Steps in that direction were made in the early 1970s, after the conclusion of agreements between East European and Middle Eastern oil-producing countries to trade equipment and other products for crude oil.

(c) Halting or at least decreasing oil exports to Western countries. The Soviets may have no choice but to do so in spite of their great need for foreign currency. In the meantime, however, signs indicate that the Soviets are doing the opposite and increasing exports.

(d) Buying oil from foreign sources. Importing Persian Gulf oil would make it possible for the USSR to increase its oil exports. This would diminish pressure to increase local production, desirable because of the great difficulty in reaching desired goals. It is cheaper in certain areas of the USSR to bring oil from the Gulf, even after the rise in prices, than from Siberia, transportation for which to the southern parts of European Russia is inadequate and expensive, and to sell West Siberian oil to European countries and East Siberian oil to Japan.

It is likely that the USSR will try every possibility, but the last choice is preferable – if convenient terms can be arranged. At this juncture, the main problem for the Soviets is that there is little to offer Gulf countries in exchange for oil. Their oil trade with Middle Eastern countries until now has been not for hard currency, but mainly for arms, some industrial products, and technical assistance. Arms are just about the only readily available commodity for export in great quantity. But, as there is a limit to Middle Eastern countries' needs and absorption capacities for military equipment, the Soviets have an interest in maintaining a certain tension that might lead to an arms race and a concomitant need for their most saleable commodity.

It is not easy to predict what the USSR oil situation will be in the 1980s because many determining factors are still unknown. Will the USSR attract foreign investment or not? How fast will the Soviet economy – and consequently the need for oil – expand? How fast will the USSR develop other energy resources? No definitive answers can be given at this stage.

Since its discovery, Persian Gulf oil has been exploited by Western oil companies, who sold it to Western countries. The USSR's occasional interest in this area was motivated by political rather than economic reasons. The Soviets believed that the West's main interest in the Middle East was its oil. Their initial entry into the area was prompted for the purpose of denying that source to the West, or at least making its use more difficult, in the belief that whatever weakened the West would strengthen the USSR. An oil price rise disadvantageous to industrialized Western countries would benefit the Soviets by offsetting their high oil production costs and encouraging development of Siberian oil deposits. The belief that what is bad for the 'capitalist world' is good for the 'socialist world' still exists. It fits well into Soviet long-term plans to destroy the economy of the West, which ultimately may be politically advantageous, but is likely to be less than efficacious with respect to immediate aims. Such destruction would probably have a negative effect on the Soviet economy as well, even if it were not to actually destroy it. For a long time, the Soviets have depended on large American, West German and Japanese loans and investments. If the price of oil rises too high, these countries may have fewer funds available for Soviet investment.

The strategic value of Middle Eastern oil and Western dependence on Gulf oil became clear after 1956, when the Soviets began taking a much greater interest in the area. The Soviets would like to see the Middle Eastern oil-producing countries develop in the following directions:

(a) Establishment of revolutionary anti-Western regimes which will maintain close relations with the Soviet Union.

(b) Nationalization of the oil fields and installations and establishment of national oil companies that will terminate assistance from Western specialists and request Soviet aid. The USSR would give them equipment and experts, provide arms and industrial goods, and receive crude oil in exchange.

It seems that the generally realistic Soviets themselves do not believe that events will unfold just their way. Even if revolutionary regimes were established, they would still continue to be interested in their countries' independence, and in selling their oil for the highest possible profit. The USSR would be able to dictate markets and conditions for oil sales only if and when those oil-producing countries became part of the 'socialist commonwealth'.

In dealing with developing countries, the Soviets prefer to provide arms, equipment and experts in exchange for local goods. Their entrance into the Middle East assumed the form of arms deals in exchange for cotton, and later also in exchange for oil. The USSR invested heavily in certain Arab countries, which produced very little oil, by providing arms, military and industrial equipment and technical assistance. These countries' debts to the USSR grew steadily, without any means of repayment. More than once, the Soviets were forced to cancel part of the debts or receive their payment in arrears. Arab oil could solve that problem for the Soviets and return at least a part of the cost of investment and loans. This arrangement succeeded in Iraq, Egypt, Syria, Algeria and other countries (of which only Iraq was a major oil producer). Arab oil-producing countries, whose relations with the USSR were previously limited or non-existent, and who bought their military and industrial equipment in Western countries, became willing to pay the Soviets in hard currency for arms which they passed on to a third party. The needs of Egypt and Syria in particular provided new opportunities for the Soviets to use their initiative to change the status quo and to widen their role in the Gulf.

The first Soviet entrance into the Gulf oil and gas market was in Iran. In January 1966, the USSR signed an agreement which provided that Iran would supply the USSR with natural gas to be paid for by Soviet construction of a steel mill in Isfahan, and provision of equipment for a trans-Iranian pipeline to transport that gas. The pipeline, 1,106 kms. long, from Khuzistan in southwest Iran to Astara on the USSR frontier, was completed in October 1970. In 1971 it carried 5,623 million cubic metres of gas. Plans exist to widen the pipeline to a capacity of 13,000 million cubic metres of gas a year, of which 10,000 million will go to the USSR and the remainder to Iran.[23]

There are also plans for a large oil pipeline from Bushire on the Gulf to Astara near the Caspian Sea, alongside the existing gas pipeline. It would pipe Gulf as well as Iranian oil to southern Russia's refining and loading facilities in the 'dying' Baku oil field and through the USSR to Western Europe. The USSR would thus serve as a land bridge between the Gulf and Europe. This would reduce the high costs of shipping and at the same time would make both producers and buyers dependent on the USSR, which could force them into accepting payment in Soviet goods, and eventually link economic dependence with Soviet political domination. However, Iran was rather unenthusiastic about this plan, foreseeing the possible consequences and therefore considered plans for pipelines leading in other directions (e.g. through Turkey).

The greatest Soviet penetration into the oil regions has occurred in Iraq. The beginnings were modest and restricted, yet it was possible to see the beginning of a process to diminish the influence of Western oil companies to the point of their complete removal. An Iraqi–Soviet agreement in December 1967 gave the Soviets their first foothold in the Iraqi oil market. In the agreement the USSR pledged to extend the necessary aid and equipment to the Iraqi National Oil Company (INOC), help them develop the Iraqi oil industry, drill wells in South Iraq and to facilitate the transportation and marketing of their products. The Soviet Union also undertook to conduct a geological survey in northern Iraq to explore the oil resources there. It was stressed that INOC was to accomplish everything – with Soviet help. Iraq would pay with shipments of crude oil.[24]

An economic and technical cooperation agreement for the development of the Iraqi oil industry in the Halfaya area, near Amara, involving about $72 million, was signed in Baghdad on June 21, 1969.[25] Another agreement signed in Moscow on July 5 of that year, provided for Soviet loans to assist Iraq in building dams, improving river navigation, erecting iron and steel works, exploiting natural gas resources and developing the North Rumayla and Ratawi oil fields (the last two to be financed by a $70 million loan repayable in crude oil).[26]

The undeveloped North Rumayla field, discovered by the Iraq Petroleum Company (IPC), was included among the Western concessions taken over by the state under General Qassim in 1960. Western oil companies (French and Italian in particular), expected to carry out the exploitation of this oil-rich field jointly with INOC. However, INOC, in what could be perceived as a victory for the Soviets, preferred to develop it themselves with Soviet assistance.

In later Soviet–Iraqi trade and aid agreements, the USSR undertook to provide equipment and technical assistance for the exploitation of Iraqi crude oil. In an agreement signed on April 8, 1971, the Soviet Union undertook to give Iraq a loan of 200 million roubles ($222 million) to be repaid in crude oil, and to finance Soviet-built projects, including an oil refinery in Mosul and an oil pipeline between Baghdad and Basra. Oil price rises were still in the future and Iraq was having economic difficulties. Isolated from other Arab and Western countries, Iraq needed Soviet aid and additional markets for its oil which relations with the USSR opened up. Production in the North Rumayla field began in April 1972. It was agreed that in 1972 the USSR would buy one million tons of crude oil from Rumayla, and in the years 1973–75 two millions a year as production of that field was estimated to increase from 5 to 18 million tons.[27]

The IPC nationalization by Iraq on June 1, 1972, and the subsequent difficulties that Iraq encountered in marketing oil in Western countries, gave the USSR an opportunity to receive more Iraqi oil on convenient terms in order to cover Iraqi debts to the USSR (mainly for arms supplied).[28] Soviet advantage from this situation, however, was limited, because of inadequate tanker tonnage and an insufficiency of conveniently located refineries.[29]

The February 28, 1973 agreement between the Iraqi government and the oil companies was described in the USSR as a great Iraqi victory.[30] According to Moscow radio, the USSR was the first country to help Iraq after the IPC nationalization by purchasing great quantities of oil and thereby frustrating the boycott of Iraqi oil by Western oil companies.[31] The fact that the Soviets did not appear to be behind the plan encouraged further nationalizations. At this stage, the Soviets were still unable to either absorb more oil or to pay for it. They apparently did not foresee what was about to happen to the oil market and still believed they were taking a risk from which they would soon gain.

The early 1973 oil crisis changed the situation completely. It soon became clear that Western oil companies were the losers and Arab oil-producing countries the winners, which made the latters' position toward friendly great powers even odder. Agreements concluded by Iraqis with the USSR at a time of weakness in 1972, when they had no other choice and were unable to sell their oil elsewhere, suddenly became less convenient because of the rise in prices and the unlimited possibilities for hard currency sales to Western countries. The Iraqis continued to sell oil to the USSR according to earlier agreements and concluded an additional one for exchanging their oil for Soviet arms and equipment. At the same time, they attempted to become less dependent on the Soviets, buying better and cheaper equipment for the development of their oil industry from the West.

The enlarged Soviet presence in Iraq aroused and exacerbated Western anxiety about Soviet attempts to control Gulf oil and brought an end to earlier Western illusions about Soviet aims in this area.

There are undoubtedly many policy-makers in the USSR who would like to achieve Soviet control of the Persian Gulf area as soon as possible, but even they do not consider it likely in the near future. For the time being, the Soviets are not able to offer oil-producing countries better terms than those they have at present; they cannot offer higher prices or hard currency, nor is it probable that they could do so in the foreseeable future. No attempts have been made by the Soviets to buy Gulf oil on a large scale, either for themselves or for their allies. Rising prices have made oil expensive for them too. Those purchases which have been made are in relatively limited quantities, mainly on the basis of trade agreements. According to Ruban Andreasyan a Soviet economist specializing in oil:

> During the last few years, as the USSR began to import oil from the Arab countries, our oil imports reached 718 million tons by 1972. It should be noted firstly, that these purchases amount to only one-tenth of our exports. Secondly, they have been made in compliance with the wishes of Arab countries who have chosen to pay with oil for Soviet credits granted as friendly assistance. Thirdly, the oil purchased from Arab countries is being supplied, with their consent, to other socialist countries.[32]

Even if the Soviets increase their purchases of Middle East oil to 100 million tons in 1980, it will still only amount to less than 10 per cent of Middle Eastern production. By then Siberian oil might be productive and the need for foreign oil be diminished. It is unlikely that the Soviets would be willing to rely on foreign countries, over which they have no full control, for their supply of a vital commodity. In order to buy Gulf oil for resale to others they would have to compete with Western countries by offering better terms. This they cannot yet do. However, they can stage conflicts between the producing countries and the West, so that they remain 'friends' and 'protectors' and as such provide arms and equipment in exchange for oil. They may also encourage local conflicts if they find it to their benefit.

In the October 1973 war of Egypt and Syria against Israel, and immediately thereafter, the USSR supplied arms and military equipment worth over $2 billion to Egypt and Syria, payment for which was made by Arab oil-producing countries. The Soviets believe that if another war breaks out in the area, there will be a renewed Arab need for Soviet arms and assistance. In the past Arab countries received Soviet arms on long-term loans, or even as grants, but this time they will be able to pay for them in hard currency or crude oil from Arab oil producers.

It is clear to the Soviets that an increase in the power of the major oil-producing countries also encourages their desire for independence – and their desire to loosen connections with the USSR. Oil producers are now able to develop a more independent foreign policy and to choose suppliers for their equipment or arms according to their wishes, which greatly strengthens their bargaining position vis-à-vis the Soviet Union.

Despite this problem, the Soviets have not forgotten their long-range strategic aim – to control the Persian Gulf area. It is only that they do not see much chance of attaining it at present and are apparently willing to wait for a more favourable opportunity.

The announcement by Arab oil producers of a drop in production and an embargo against the United States, as well as other countries, which followed the October 1973 Arab–Israeli war, was enthusiastically received by the Soviet information media. The Arabs were advised to continue using 'oil as a weapon' against Israel and 'her overseas protectors', in the hope that an exacerbation of American–Arab relations would foster closer Soviet–Arab ties.

Although the Soviets tried to manipulate the 'oil war' for their own benefit, they were not unaware that they had no hand in its implementation or operation and could do little more than respond to an existing situation. Such a response accorded neatly with their policy of advancing only to the brink of the abyss, of walking a tightrope with great care. They took no active part in this political development; no one requested their intervention or even consulted them; any offers of help by the Soviet media were ignored.

The media encouraged the Arabs to continue their boycott, asserted its legality, and promised unwavering Soviet support. The Western countries felt they had little choice but to be placatory because they also feared Soviet intervention on the Arab side; the mere existence of the Soviet Union assured the Arabs that no one would dare assail them with nineteenth-century style gunboat diplomacy.

The USSR knew how important Middle East oil was to Western countries; if the latter were to be pushed hard enough, and confronted with a situation in which they had nothing to lose, they would react with force if necessary.

If the Arab oil producers had requested Soviet assistance, it would have become apparent that the Soviets had no intention of intervening; their words and promises were only propaganda. That the West did not react was interpreted as a sign of weakness, of disputes among the Western powers and as fear of a Soviet response.

Soviet broadcasts to Arab countries reiterated that the Americans were prepared to resort to military force if the oil embargo continued. Saudi Arabia and Kuwait made it known that they would blow up their oil wells should the attempt be made. Several versions of this story were broadcast by the Soviet media.[33] Despite this dissemination, however, it was quite clear to Soviet oil specialists, as well as to Soviet leaders that these threats were not serious, as any damage inflicted could be repaired in short order. As the Soviets were convinced the West would intervene (the USSR would not have hesitated to do so in a similar situation, and could not comprehend why any power capable of acting did not) one might see their propaganda as a cover-up for their own inactivity.

The presence of American naval units in the western part of the Indian Ocean was bitterly resented by the Soviet Union, and was cited as proof of the Soviet allegation that the Americans were supporting the oil companies and therefore had dispatched the Seventh Fleet vessels to seize the oil fields if necessary. However, a Soviet broadcast stated, the Arabs were able to defend themselves.[34] It is significant that Arab defence capability was stressed without any suggestion that the Soviet Union would offer active support.

The Arabs were advised to withdraw their oil revenues from Western banks and to invest those funds in joint Soviet–Arab companies to which the Soviets would contribute equipment and technical know-how.[35] There were recurrent calls for the nationalization of Western oil companies: the Arabs could do as they wished with Arab oil.[36] Those countries which had nationalized their oil resources were making major strides in production. Iraq's North

Rumayla field development was proof that oil could be produced without foreign companies; the Western boycott of Iraqi oil had failed because of Soviet aid to the Iraqi oil industry.[37]

The Soviet public was repeatedly told that the energy crisis was the outcome of the policies of the monopolistic oil companies and of the capitalist system; they were witness to the efficiency of the USSR's socialist economic planning – as opposed to capitalist laissez-faire which led to frequent crises. Oil companies, declared the Soviet media, should be phased out altogether as they become rich by exploiting both oil producers and consumers:[38] direct contact between producers and consumers ought to be established in spite of American attempts to prevent it.[39]

In disregard of the effect that the oil crisis was having on Western European economies, the Soviet media continued to maintain that Western Europe was not dissatisfied with the situation because it offered independence from American middlemen. France, for instance, came in for repeated praise for having established direct contacts with Arab oil producers; Britain, it was claimed, would follow suit.[40] However, beneath their benign approval of the turn of events, an old Soviet fear surfaced that the oil crisis might drive Western Europe toward greater unity, and the Soviets energetically undermined all attempts to bring the industrialized countries together.

The Washington energy conference of February 11–18, 1974, sponsored by the United States with the participation of Western oil consumers, received much attention and criticism from the Soviet media which stressed, with particular satisfaction, the lack of unity between Western countries (especially French dissension), in the hope that the rift might grow.[41] To the Arabs, the conference was depicted as a plot against them, as testified by the fact that they had not been invited.[42] The USSR suggested convening a 'counter-conference' to include the Arab states, the USSR and her allies.[43]

The principal aim of the Washington conference, as presented by the Soviets, was to preserve American political and economic hegemony over Western Europe and Japan. The Americans were also said to have failed in their purpose. After the conference, nevertheless, the Arabs were told that the West was attempting to establish a united front against them. It was in the Arab interest, therefore, to strengthen relations with their 'natural ally', the USSR.[44]

The Soviet attitude towards the Arab–Israeli conflict hardened in the second half of February 1974. Increasingly, the Arabs were told to take a more militant stand against the Israelis and the American-sponsored Arab–Israeli negotiations. The Egyptian–Israeli separation of forces early in 1974 had brought an improvement in American–Egyptian relations and a corresponding Egyptian movement away from the USSR. Once again it became clear to the Soviets that it was easier to consolidate their position in the Arab world during times of crisis than in the midst of negotiation, with its emphasis on economic reconstruction and development.

Because the Arab oil embargo against the United States was so apparent an obstacle to American–Arab rapprochement, the Soviet Union exerted its propaganda efforts to convince the Arabs to maintain the embargo and to expand their struggle against Western oil companies so as to effect their nationalization.[45] Although this type of propaganda was intended as a hint to the Americans that the USSR would not permit any deals in the Middle East without its participation and consent, the Soviets were careful not to go too far in their threats, lest they endangered Soviet–American détente.

The Arabic broadcasts of the allegedly unofficial Moscow 'Radio Peace and Progress' station were particularly sharp in attacking the United States and advocating continuation of the oil embargo.[46] The United States, it was said, had no interest in solving the Middle East crisis but only wished to mediate between the Arabs and Israel in order to persuade the Arabs to lift their embargo, without receiving in return the land occupied by Israel. The Arabs therefore should resume their oil supply to the United States only after a total Israeli withdrawal.[47] 'If some Arab leaders are today ready to surrender in the face of American pressure to lift the ban before (Arab) demands are met, they are taking the risk of challenging the entire Arab world and all the world's progressive forces.'[48] This Soviet broadcast was veiled criticism of Egyptian President Anwar as-Sadat, who advocated terminating the embargo, and of Saudi Arabia's King Faysal, who discreetly supported Sadat's stand.

The Soviet media campaigned particularly vigorously for an anti-American oil embargo when the Organization of Arab Petroleum Exporting Countries (OAPEC) met in Tripoli (mid-March 1974) to discuss the question. Despite President Sadat's earlier protestations that American policy in the Middle East was becoming more favourable to the Arabs, the Soviets tried to persuade the Arabs that American policy was unaltered, that the United States should prove its goodwill and support the Arabs *before* the embargo was lifted.

An end to the embargo would deprive the Arabs of an 'effective weapon', and the United States might see it as Arab surrender, Moscow radio said. The embargo had not yet achieved its aim: 'Lifting the embargo without . . . specific guarantees that the crisis would be subsequently resolved would result in a freezing of the situation in the Middle East.'[49] Dispatches from the Tripoli conference gave detailed reports of those who called for a continuation of the embargo but did not mention those who wanted its discontinuance.[50]

The lifting of the oil embargo by Arab oil ministers in Vienna on March 18, 1974 was masterminded by Saudi Arabia, the largest oil producer, which felt that its continuation might evoke an increasing radicalization of the Arab world that would endanger the Saudi regime, increase Soviet influence in the area and hasten the development of alternative energy sources to the detriment of Arab bargaining power. Soviet commentators called the decision 'premature', and argued that the Arabs were depriving themselves of a weapon which they might need again.[51]

The Arabs were encouraged by the Soviets to continue the oil embargo against the United States while the Soviets themselves were selling oil products to America. According to the US customs records 'since the first of the year', four tankers loaded with Soviet petroleum products docked in New York and New Jersey ports. Soviet petroleum shipments 'began long before the Arab boycott was initiated' and the Soviets showed no intention of stopping them. In some cases the ships which carried American wheat brought back Soviet oil to the United States. The Soviets were said to have fulfilled 'all their contractual obligations'.[52]

Once the embargo was lifted calls to renew it were quite frequently heard in Soviet broadcasts to the Arabs. Radio 'Peace and Progress' (in Arabic) said on May 16, 1974, that 'it is not surprising that the Arab states should raise the issue of the resumption of the oil embargo. Although some may say that the resumption of the use of the oil weapon will only succeed when all the Arab states join the oil embargo, the fact is that the world of today is in constant need of oil, and therefore the embargo will be successful and lead to the expected results even when it is limited to a few states considered to be the most important oil-producing countries'. In the existing situation in the Middle East 'Arab cooperation based on animosity towards Israel and imperialism' would lead to a renewal of the oil embargo which was certain to yield better and faster results than cooperation with the United States.

A Moscow radio broadcast in Arabic (August 20, 1974) typifies the way the Soviets presented the matter to the Arabs: 'America's profits from the exploitation of Arab oil amount to billions of dollars annually. Monopolies from other capitalist countries draw fantastic profits. But the extension of the Arab national liberation movement which enjoys the support of the socialist community has recently greatly helped the Gulf oil-producing countries in strengthening their positions against oil imperialism.' The oil-producing countries' struggle 'now aims at securing full sovereignty of the oil-producing countries over their resources . . . the role of Arab oil is growing in both the economic and political fields. And it is in the Arab interest to see that this role grows further in the future'.

The 'energy crisis' and oil embargo served Soviet aims well; it rent the 'capitalist world' and impeded an improvement in Arab–American relations. Nothing could please the Soviets more than having an American oil company unable to supply oil to the US navy, and American companies forbidden, at least officially, to send oil to their own country.

As far as possible, the Soviets tried to prevent the lifting of the embargo, seeking support from their 'progressive' Arab allies (who did not keep the embargo themselves). But the Soviets, unlike the Saudis, did not seem to understand that a prolongation of the embargo might provoke more determined American measures, and that its very existence strengthened those in the administration who opposed making any concessions whatsoever to the Arabs and were determined to find alternative energy sources which would make the United States and, ultimately, Western Europe, independent of Arab oil.

It must be stressed that in spite of the massive, emotional propaganda efforts, actual Soviet influence on the oil embargo was minimal. Increased power and wealth made the Arabs politically much more independent than previously. Soviet propaganda had little influence on the Arab rulers, whose only criteria were their own interests. It was clear to them that the Soviets, in accordance with their brinkmanship policy, did not care at all to be directly involved in a conflict with the United States. Therefore, despite the apparent offers (which conservative anti-communist oil producers did not wish to accept) the rulers knew they could not rely on Soviet support.

CHAPTER II

Russia and the Middle East

The Tsarist Period

The Russian state was born in the vicinity of Moscow and gradually expanded in all directions. A transient frontier, very similar to that in the United States, developed – a frontier of the hunter, fisherman, trader, miner, bandit, freebooter, military conqueror and colonizer.[1] Unlike Western Europeans who were accustomed to venturing on far-flung overseas colonization, the Russians expanded into contiguous lands where they intermingled with the native population. 'Scratch a Russian and you will catch a Tatar', goes an old saying.

Russian history has been greatly influenced by its geography, its enormous steppes and plains – vast areas without natural barriers which allowed the penetration of nomads from the east and the south. The defence of such an area and the establishment of secure frontiers were achieved only after acquiring control over the entire plain, the main entrances to it and the mountains around it.

In the campaign against the Ottomans during the eighteenth century, Russia won the entire northern shore of the Black Sea, which gave it egress to the south. Simultaneously, Russia began a lengthy war in the East which eventually enabled movement south of the Caucasus Mountains. By 1820, the Russian frontier had reached the Araxes River, and was expanded no further until the occupation of the Caucasus area was completed after 1860.

The long wars with Turkey and Persia aroused Russian interest in the countries lying south of her adversaries. The Russians examined existing local separatist movements, as well as the possibility of encouraging the growth of such movements specifically supporting Russian policy. In 1809, for instance, the Russian Foreign Ministry requested its Transcaucasian military detachment to send to the recalcitrant Sulayman, Pasha of Baghdad, an official 'who must try

c

to exploit the Pasha's wish "for a complete separation from the Porte" and (convince him) to act against Persia and (who will) promise him Russian protection'.[2]

This incident, although inconsequential, was one of the first Russian moves in the direction of the Persian Gulf, an area that the British considered within their sphere of influence. Further Russian incursions were watched carefully by the British, who saw their own interests threatened. For the time being the threat was more potential than real.

British suspicion of Russian intentions increased as the Russians continued their conquests in Central Asia in the second half of the nineteenth century. Several British statesmen now considered this expansion a threat to British India.[3] In fact, no evidence exists of any serious Russian intent to invade India. To implement such a plan the Russians would have needed a much larger force in that area than they could spare and they would have had to overcome tremendous logistic difficulties. Some Russian military commanders on the southern peripheries might have contemplated further southward advances and even dreamed about marching to the Indian Ocean,[4] but their views were generally not shared by their superiors, less so by the Russian capital. Russian activity in the direction of the Gulf was intended to influence British policies in Europe or the Near East, and in particular, to coerce the British into reducing their support of Turkey. In addition there were border areas of Russia and Persia in which the Russians had a particular interest as a sort of sphere of influence. Even though at that time Russia had no intention of annexing these areas nor of controlling them, it tried to make certain other countries (Britain especially) did not get them either. Britain intended to move northward. The Russian menace strengthened the British resolve to arrest the Russian southward advance and keep the Russians as distant as possible from India. This situation gave local rulers (e.g. in Afghanistan) room for manoeuvre, made further advances from either direction difficult, and established a kind of buffer zone between the two large powers, but did not apply to Persia where the Russian presence and influence increased continuously during the nineteenth century. The 1828 Treaty of Turkmanchai ceded to Russia the provinces of Erevan and Nakhichevan, imposed a heavy indemnity on Persia and forced it to grant commercial privileges and extraterritorial rights to Russian subjects; Persia ceased to be an independent power. This marked the beginning of

Russian economic and political penetration into Persia, especially in the northern parts adjacent to Russia.

The organization of a Cossack Brigade in Persia in 1879 was one of the results of the Russian penetration. This Brigade was trained by Russian officers who dealt directly with the Ministry of War at St Petersburg and became, as the most efficient military force in Persia an extremely important political tool.[5]

No less important for Russia was the establishment of a communications network to advance its plan in Central Asia. One of the greatest difficulties in this area was the transfer of soldiers and equipment over great distances and inaccessible areas.

In order to reach Central Asia and farther along the Persian border, consolidate their gains, and be able to control their newly-acquired territories, the Russians built a number of railways. The first line, which was formally opened in 1888, ran from the Caspian Sea eastwards; from Krasnovodsk, via Ashkhabad to Merv, Samarkand and Tashkent, and continued to Kokand and Andizhan. A branch-line from Merv to the Afghan border to Kushka was opened in 1898. The western side of the Caspian could be reached by a railway line running from Moscow to Baku. A more direct line to Central Asia, Orenburg–Tashkent, was completed in 1906. The Trans-Caspian line was extended to Juifa, on the Persian border and from there, during World War I, to Tabriz.

The extension of Russia's railway system to the Persian border contributed much to the expansion of Russian influence in Persia at the close of the nineteenth century. In turn, the Russians considered the expansion of the system beyond Russian territories through Persia to the Gulf, to Bandar Abbas, Bushire or Shahbahar farther east of the coast of the Arabian Sea. Bandar Abbas received special attention because the Russians wanted a port in that vicinity, or at least rights to use the existing facility. A railway to a port in the Persian Gulf or Arab Gulf of the Arabian Sea could provide Russia with even more control over Persia and greater influence on the neighbouring countries. It would also serve Russian ships which passed through the Suez Canal and the north Indian Ocean to the Far East, and to its Russian areas in particular. Even after laying the Trans-Siberian railway, in 1891, the Russians needed sea transportation through the Indian Ocean because the line could not carry all the freight from European Russia to Far Eastern Russia.

However, plans for a Gulf port and the railway line to it originated at unofficial or lower-level government strata and were generally not approved by the higher echelons. The lower strata considered Persia primarily an area for manoeuvre against the British. Their priorities were, on the one hand, along the traditional line of advance westward to the Turkish straits and, on the other, toward the Far East, where they wished to extend and develop the Trans-Siberian railway and add branches. As resources were limited, those who saw many possibilities in the Far East tried to stop development in the direction of the Persian Gulf, arguing that strong British resistance could be expected.

The problem was brought before the Russian government by the Head of the Asian Department in the Foreign Ministry as early as February 1890. He objected to the construction of a railway from the Russian border through Persia to the Persian Gulf because, he argued, uninterrupted movement along such a line would require continuous security. Such security, he contended, could not be ensured and the farther one moved from the Russian frontier, the more difficult it would be to maintain. Even so, he called for establishment in the Gulf of 'a Russian military naval station, strong enough to face English rivalry in this distant country and to command the respect of the littoral population'.[6] No decision was adopted on the matter at the time, only one year before construction began on the long-planned Trans-Siberian railway in 1891.

In 1896 China agreed to allow construction of a railway across Manchuria, shortening the long route from Irkutsk to Vladivostok and opening many opportunities for Russia in this area. A railway boom developed in the western, more populated, parts of European Russia, bringing with it a rise in the growth of Russian industry.

The proliferation of Russian railway construction companies prompted Russian entrepreneurs and contractors to use their experience and skills in construction projects in other countries. By 1898 a Russian subject, Count Vladimir Kapnist, had applied to the Ottoman government for a concession to construct a railway from the Syrian port of Tripoli to Kuwait, via Homs, Baghdad and Basra. The construction of that line would have given Russia many political advantages, by actually turning the whole area through which it passed over to Russian control, an arrangement reminiscent of the Manchurian railway. Count Kapnist could not, however, secure enough private Russian capital and sought British and French cooperation. The British Foreign Office strongly advised against it and exerted great pressure to prevent the construction of the line, which contributed to the failure of the project.[7]

German plans for what came to be known as the Baghdad railway met with more success.[8] On November 25, 1899, the Ottoman Porte granted the Germans rights to construct a railway from Konia to Baghdad. Initially the Germans were encouraged by the British because a German entrance into Turkey and a modern system of communications would strengthen Turkey, counter Russian expansionist schemes at the expense of the Ottoman Empire, drive a wedge between Germany and Russia, and effect German–Russian competition.

The German–Baghdad railway plans aroused much concern in St Petersburg. Russian newspapers expressed suspicion of an English–German secret agreement which would give Britain a free hand in Africa and Germany discretion over Asia Minor.[9] The Russians believed that the railway would stretch through southern Persia to Baluchistan, thus impeding Russian access to the Persian Gulf. Another concern was that the railway might enable Germany to develop Mesopotamia into a granary for Europe that would compete with Russia's important agricultural exports, on which it depended for purchases of capital goods.[10]

The Russian press published opinions that since the Germans were building a railway to the Persian Gulf from the West, Russia should immediately begin to build a road to the Gulf from the north. The Russian government itself decided not to support these plans for financial and political reasons. Moreover, it felt that the construction of a road connecting northern Persia, a traditional market for Russian goods, with the Gulf, might open the region to British commerce and encourage the British to build a railway from the south to northern Persia.

In a review of his country's policy in Asia, Foreign Minister, Count M. N. Muravyov, in January 1900, referred to his government's decision not to build a road to Persia and occupy a port on the Persian Gulf. On the latter point, he said that he saw no justification for occupying ports 'whose defence could not be fully ensured. It might be added that the building of strategic positions and coaling stations, which are divided by long distances from the operational base, disperses the forces of the country, and costs so much, that the advantages in most cases are not worth their material sacrifices.' He opposed a division of Persia into Russian and British spheres of influence. Northern Persia was already under Russian influence and 'inaccessible' to foreigners. A division would only stop Russian advances into the South.

> The Head of the Naval Ministry commented on February 14 (27), 1900:
> I fully agree about the uselessness of our acquisition of coaling stations or any bases outside the Empire's borders which do not justify the expense of their fortification and fleet maintenance, and without which they would only become an easy prey for the enemy.[11]

While the Head of the Russian Naval Ministry was writing about the 'uselessness' of acquiring distant coaling stations or bases, a small Russian gunboat was anchored off Bandar Abbas. The commander ordered coal from Bombay, took some aboard and wanted to leave the rest in port. As a matter of course, Russian guards would have remained to guard the coal, and thus, 'create a nucleus store from which a coaling station might develop'. The local governor therefore refused permission to leave any coal.[12] Russian warships continued to tour the Gulf, but no attempts were made to acquire a footing there.[13] This incident was probably an exception, made perhaps on the ship captain's own initiative or as an attempt to test local or British reactions. In fact British naval supremacy made the Gulf a British preserve and obviated any Russian plans to enter it – assuming such plans existed.

The defeat of Russia in its war with Japan in 1905, domestic instability, the 1905 revolution, German penetration in the Near East, economic difficulties, all contributed to a Russian reappraisal of its foreign policy, and, to a lesser degree, its view of Britain as a competitor, if not enemy. On the other hand, Russia had no desire to see Germany as Turkey's protector, which would limit the possibility of realizing the age-old hope of acquiring at least partial control of the Straits which connect the Black Sea with the Mediterranean, and Turkey in general. Gradually, a Russo-British rapprochement evolved, reaching its peak with the signing of the 1907 convention between both countries. Among its provisions was the partition of Persia into British and Russian spheres of influence with a neutral zone in between. The richest northern part was in the Russian sphere. Bandar Abbas and eastward, including Afghanistan, were in the British sphere. The Gulf area westward was in the neutral area.[14]

The Persian Gulf area descended still lower in the Russian scale of priorities. Russian interest and efforts in the Near and Middle East were concentrated in the direction of the Turkish Straits and upon the Ottoman Empire. It expressed itself, inter alia, during World War I, in the negotiations and secret treaties between Russia and its wartime allies, Great Britain and France. Russian plans to reach the Gulf were postponed for more opportune times.

CHAPTER III

Soviet Regime – First Stages (1917–1947)

Russia's old regime ended in March 1917. A few months later, on November 7,[1] the Bolsheviks came to power and proclaimed a Soviet, 'proletarian-socialist' regime.

The new regime's first priorities were the fight for survival, consolidation of power, and retention of all, or at least most, of the areas which had belonged to Russia before the revolution. Attention was focused on Europe – the regime dealt with the 'East' only in order to influence developments in Europe; the main Soviet 'Eastern' policy was intended to create difficulties for the colonial powers (and Britain in particular) so as to distract them from fighting the new Soviet regime.[2]

In the first years of the new regime attempts were made by Soviet Russia to establish contacts with anti-colonial movements and to develop communist parties in 'Eastern' countries. These efforts met with little success. In most countries such parties as there were existed chiefly on paper, had only a limited number of followers and little, if any, influence. They were nonetheless advised to advocate a 'two-stage revolution' formula. The first 'bourgeois democratic' stage, led by the 'national bourgeoisie', was to achieve national independence and the communists were to be a part of a wide 'anti-colonial and anti-imperialist' coalition. Subsequently, the communists would increase their role in the coalition, thus initiating the second stage of the 'socialist' revolution, in which 'the workers' and peasants' movements' would seize power from the 'bourgeoisie'. The theory presumed the universal existence of 'a class-conscious proletariat' and a strong local communist party. But in most Middle Eastern countries there were almost no communists at all, much less a proletariat. The chances for these developments were very slim.

Soviet leaders appeared aware of the problem, even if they did not publicly acknowledge it, and policy differed for East and West. In

Western Europe, the Soviets, despite trying to establish state-to-state relations, still supported revolutionary movements which acted against those states' regimes. The Soviet government assured its southern neighbours, on the other hand, that it was not against them but was very ready to help them. The main Soviet objective in Iran and Afghanistan was to eliminate British influence and create a buffer zone of the two states between Soviet territory and British India, hoping to make them dependent on Soviet Russia and use them as springboards for further Soviet advancement.[3]

According to a Soviet writer in 1918, a revolution in Persia might become 'the key to a revolution in the whole East'. Just as Egypt and the Suez Canal were the key to British domination of the East, so Persia was 'the "Suez Canal" of the revolution'. By 'turning the political focus of the revolution toward Persia, the whole strategic value of the Suez Canal would be lost'.[4] However, while the Russians were preoccupied with internal affairs, the British negotiated the Anglo-Persian treaty of 1919 which recognized Persia's independence and territorial unity, revoked the 1907 Anglo-Russian treaty and made Persia de facto dependent on Britain.

The Soviets countered the British agreement with the signing, on February 26, 1921, of a Soviet–Persian Friendship Treaty whereby Soviet Russia renounced all Tsarist privileges, recognized Persia's sovereignty and agreed to evacuate its troops from Persia. Nevertheless, the Treaty included a clause that Soviet troops might return to Persia should a third power threaten Persia or transform Persian territory 'into a base for military operations against Russia'.[5] This clause served as the basis for Soviet intervention in Persia (which had changed its name in the meantime to Iran) in August 1941, to prevent its occupation by Germany.

A special interest was shown by Soviet Russia in the Red Sea area. The Soviet state's isolation and the boycott of it by many countries, made the Soviet Union anxious to establish relations with any state ready to do so. It had also an interest in maintaining a presence in an area considered a British sphere of influence and important to British interests, especially as the British government appeared to be following a strong anti-Soviet policy.

The first diplomatic relations with an Arab country were established with the Hejaz in 1924. The Soviets attached an unwarranted importance to this move, assuming that because of its Muslim holy places, the Hussayn would be influential over other Muslim states as well as over the Muslim population of the USSR. The British, and other powers who had previously attributed great importance to Hussayn had by then realized their mistake and were aware of the limitations of Hussayn's power even in his own country. At this time relations between Hussayn and the British were strained, as Hussayn refused to recognize the peace agreements. As Wahhabi pressure grew, he found himself almost entirely isolated and friendless. The Soviets hoped that developing relations with him would present them with an opportunity to break into a British sphere of influence and pose a challenge to Britain.[6]

The Hejaz was conquered by Ibn Sa'ud who became 'King of Hejaz, Sultan of Najd and its Dependencies'. In pursuance of its previous policy, the USSR was the first foreign power to accord him recognition. In 1927 two Soviet trade delegations visited Hejaz. The British saw a danger to their position in this Soviet activity and exerted pressure to stop it. A Soviet trade delegation which visited Hejaz in 1928 met with failure. Nonetheless, an agreement was signed on August 2, 1931, which provided for a Soviet shipment to Saudi Arabia of 100,000 crates of petrol and kerosene. Prince Faysal (subsequent ruler of Saudi Arabia), a son of Ibn Sa'ud served as a sort of minister of foreign affairs, and visited the USSR in May 1932. The Soviets unsuccessfully tried to use that occasion to sign a trade agreement.[7]

The initiation of relations between the USSR and Yemen in 1928 also had an anti-British character. The Imam Yahya of Yemen appeared opposed to British influence, in Aden in particular, and his moves to establish relations with the USSR, and enable the Soviets to penetrate his country (albeit on a small scale) were clearly directed against Britain.

In May 1928, a Soviet trading ship loaded with Soviet goods visited Hudayda. A 'Treaty of Friendship and Trade' between the USSR and Yemen was signed on November 1, 1928. The USSR sold Yemen kerosene and other commodities and provided medical aid. The Soviet Union also helped Yemen to establish ties with Germany, with whom the USSR enjoyed good relations at this time.[8] These activities in Saudi Arabia and Yemen facilitated the Soviet Union's establishment of trade relations with Eritrea (then under Italian control), and Ethiopia.[9]

Though limited in scope, Soviet relations with the Red Sea countries in the 1920s and early 1930s were part of an attempt to attack 'imperialism' from an unexpected direction, undermine its power, and erode its ability to fight the Soviet state. Policy changed in the mid-1930s with the rise of Nazi Germany, which proclaimed its militant anti-communism and enmity to the Soviet Union; moreover, a certain improvement had occurred in relations with Britain which the Soviets desired to foster. The minimal commercial and diplomatic Soviet activity in the Red Sea area was significant insofar as it furthered Soviet purposes, but once a danger was seen in Europe, it was there that the Soviets concentrated all their efforts. A presence in a peripheral area lost importance.

Developments in Central and Eastern Europe, which directly affected their security, remained of the highest importance to the Soviets. In negotiations in 1940 between Soviet and German representatives, the Germans tried to draw Soviet attention to the area 'south of the national territory of the Soviet Union in the direction of the Indian Ocean' and thereby divert the USSR from claims to territories in Europe which the Germans considered their 'lebensraum'.

In a conversation between Hitler and Molotov (then Soviet Premier and Foreign Minister) in Berlin on November 13, 1940, Hitler said that after the German conquest of England and the division of the British Empire 'there would be for Russia an access to the ice-free and really open ocean' and that 'even now' Germany recognized the 'Asiatic area' to the south of the Soviet Union as 'Russia's sphere of influence'. Molotov, however, preferred to discuss the future of Bulgaria, the Turkish Straits and other more immediate issues. The same attitude was evident in a meeting on the same day between German Foreign Minister von Ribbentrop and Molotov.[10]

A secret protocol to a draft agreement between Germany, Italy, Japan and the Soviet Union prepared by the Germans, defined the spheres of the territorial aspirations of each participant as 'apart from the territorial revision in Europe to be carried out at the conclusion of Peace'. Accordingly, Germany's 'territorial aspirations centre in the territories of Central Africa'; Japan's 'in the area of Eastern Asia to the south of the Island Empire of Japan'. The Soviet Union 'declares that its territorial aspirations centre south of the national territory of the Soviet Union in the direction of the Indian Ocean'.[11]

Apparently the draft was the topic of a conversation between Molotov and the German Ambassador in Moscow, von Schulenburg, on November 26, 1940. Von Schulenburg reported to the German Foreign Office that Molotov stated that the Soviet Government was prepared to 'accept the draft of the Four Power Pact' on the following conditions:

(1) 'The establishment of a base for land and naval forces of the USSR with the range of the Bosporus and the Dardanelles by means of a long-term lease' in the Turkish Straits.

(2) 'Provided that the area south of Batum and Baku in the general direction of the Persian Gulf is recognized as the centre of the aspirations of the Soviet Union'.[12]

Though the German proposals were supposed to distract attention from Europe, the Soviets remained attentive to Europe, perceiving that their main interests lay there rather than in the Middle East. Hitler decided to discontinue negotiations with them, and a month later, on December 18, 1940, he issued his 'Operation Barbarossa' order to attack the Soviet Union.[13]

The German attack began on June 22, 1941. The number of Germans in Iran and the influence they brought to bear were seen as a danger to both Britain and the USSR. On August 25, 1941, British and Soviet troops marched into Iran, and as had happened before World War I, Iran again was divided into British and Soviet areas, with the Soviets occupying the northern provinces. The pro-German Riza Shah was forced to abdicate and was succeeded by his son, Muhammad Riza Pahlevi.

During the war years, Iran's importance grew as a corridor for American military supplies to the USSR. The Trans-Iranian Railway from Bandar Shahpur on the Persian Gulf to Bandar Shah on the Caspian Sea, completed in 1938, became the main channel of supply for that route.[14] This was the line planned by Russia many years earlier to the Persian Gulf and India.

The main Soviet interest remained in Europe. Only once they were free of the German threat could the Soviets pursue their old plans to expand southward, ensuring their access to the Indian Ocean. During the later stages of the war, diplomatic relations were established between the USSR and Ethiopia (July 1943), Egypt (August 1943), Syria (July 1944), Lebanon (August 1944), and Iraq (September 1944). When negotiations on the fate of the Italian colonies (Tripolitania, Libya, Somaliland and Eritrea) were conducted, the USSR expressed a wish to place them under Soviet trusteeship. The matter was referred to at the summit meetings of allied leaders in

Yalta and Potsdam by the Soviets but was strongly opposed by Britain.[15]

Later, at the Conference of Foreign Ministers in Paris in April 1946, Molotov formally requested that the USSR be given control over the port of Massawa in Eritrea, but this was rejected. The Soviets demanded the Turkish areas of Kars and Ardahan, which Russia had captured from Turkey in 1878 and held until World War I. Claims were also made for Turkish Armenia and Georgia, which constituted a greater part of Turkey and reached up to its borders with Iraq and Iran.[16] The Soviet pressure was counter-productive in that it drove Turkey to seek closer relations with the Western powers.

Soviet military forces remained in Iran after the War, since the Soviets planned to retain control of northern Iran. In December 1945 they established the 'Autonomous Republic of Azerbijan' and a 'Kurdish People's Republic'. But once the Soviet troops were withdrawn from Iran because of strong American protest (May 1946), the Azerbijani and Kurdish republics collapsed. Moreover, even the Soviet–Iranian agreement to establish a joint company to exploit oil in north Iran was not ratified by the Iranian Majlis. In sum, Soviet attempts to exploit their position and establish a foothold in the environs of the Persian Gulf and the Indian Ocean met with no success.

CHAPTER IV

Limited Soviet Successes (1940–late 1950s)

At the end of World War II the USSR emerged as a leading world power. Turkey had long been a target of Russian expansion. It controlled land, sea and air routes from the USSR to the Mediterranean, the Middle East and the Persian Gulf. Immediately after the war the Soviets asked for a base on the Dardanelles. This would have changed the regime of the Straits set up by the Montreux Convention of 1936, by proposing, inter alia, that the Straits be jointly defended by the USSR and Turkey and that some Turkish territory be ceded to the Soviet Union.[1] At the same time the Soviets tried to outflank Turkey by attempts to bring pro-Russian forces to power in Greece.

Greece and Turkey were unable to withstand Soviet pressure alone. Britain, who had previously protected them, was unable to maintain the shield, and the United States replaced Britain. A so-called 'Truman Doctrine' of aid to Greece and Turkey was proclaimed in March 1947.[2] In early 1949, the North Atlantic Treaty Organization (NATO) was established, and included among its members Greece and Turkey.

Iran was no less a major Soviet target as the nearest pathway to open sea for the Soviet Central Asian and Trans-Caucasus republics. Obversely, Iran could be utilized by the enemies of the USSR as a 'rear door' to the Soviet territories. Iran's northern frontier was close to the Baku oil wells and the Baku–Batum pipeline where a hostile presence might threaten the USSR's most important industrial areas of the Volga–Don and the southern Urals.

During the 1951 Anglo-Iranian oil crisis, Soviet information media strongly supported the Iranian position and criticized the British and Americans for their counteraction. Soviet representatives even hinted at their country's readiness to provide markets and technicians to overcome the Western boycott. The situation in Iran appealed to the Soviets although it came at a most inconvenient time for them; in the midst of the Korean war, they could not afford another confrontation with Western powers. The disappointment of their previous attempts to interfere in internal Iranian affairs was still fresh in their minds and the Soviets were not entirely sure that Dr Mossadegh would not replace the British with the Americans. The Soviets decided, therefore, to avoid direct involvement and act through local communists, the Tudeh party and communist-inspired 'front organizations'. The Tudeh widened its role in Iranian politics, and at one stage of the crisis was not far from assuming power.

In mid-August 1953, the Shah had to leave the country. Though the forces that stood behind Dr Mossadegh were mainly nationalist, they were confused and disunited. Had the monarchy been overthrown, the Tudeh undoubtedly would have played a major, if not a leading role, in the government of Iran. However, shortly afterwards, the Shah was returned to power by a coup staged by pro-Western General Fazlollah Zahedi, who brought an end to Soviet hopes. Iran had been close to falling under Soviet influence but the Tudeh party leadership also hesitated to seize power despite the arrival of a long-awaited opportunity, with Iran's regime close to collapse in August 1953. The Soviet leadership was then preoccupied with internal struggles for power. Its leading members had already come to the conclusion that the USSR's Middle East policy had been in error, but had not yet decided upon another; Soviet hesitation played its part in the Tudeh failure of nerve.[3]

Great changes were evident in Soviet policy toward the Afro-Asian states after Stalin's death in March 1953 and after the April 1955 Bandung Afro-Asian Conference in particular.[4] The former doctrinaire attitude of 'who is not with us is against us' was replaced by the far more pragmatic approach of 'who is not against us is with us'. Opposition to Western powers, whether nationalist or even religious in inspiration was considered 'anti-imperialist' and 'national liberation movements' received both praise and support.

Changes in American policy also appeared. The Eisenhower administration, which took office in January 1953, and its chief spokesman on foreign policy, Secretary of State John Foster Dulles, advocated a more vigorous policy in relation to the USSR. The war in Korea, just ended, proved to the US that its 'containment' policy was impractical. Reappraisal of defence policy created a new one which placed greater emphasis on the Strategic Air Force's nuclear air power. Thus, a chain of bases around the USSR, located in US-allied states came into being and comprised the so-called 'northern tier' (Turkey and Iran in particular) integral to Western defence plans. On February 24, 1955 a Western-sponsored mutual defence treaty known as the Baghdad Pact was signed between Turkey and Iraq.[5] It was joined in the same year by Pakistan, Iran and also by Britain.

The Baghdad Pact evoked considerable anxiety in the USSR. The Soviets felt it endangered vital parts of their country and exposed its south-central areas, the USSR's 'soft underbelly', to Western pen-etration, even more so than in Europe where they were protected by a buffer zone of satellite states. Moreover, the Soviets had just decided to begin a new policy of penetration and activity in the Afro-Asian countries. The Baghdad Pact looked like a Western attempt to stop it and prevent a Soviet advance in that direction.

The Soviets looked for ways to terminate this Pact (by both threats and offers of generous technical and other aid) and circum-vent it by establishing a presence to the south. The Soviet–Egyptian arms deal made public in September 1955 (as an Egyptian–Czechoslovakian deal) was a step in the circumvention process. Negotiations had actually begun much earlier – the first contacts were already made in 1954 (not, as the Egyptians used to say, only after Israel's raid in the Gaza Strip in February 1955).[6] A similar arms deal was later signed between the USSR and Syria. The Soviet aim was to outflank the Baghdad Pact. As early as 1955, there were signs that the Soviet Union was already considering Egypt an ideal tool with which to penetrate the countries of the Third World, including those of the Arabian Peninsula.

One of the countries in which the Soviets were interested was Saudi Arabia, where they had attempted to cultivate a friendship before World War II. Until 1957 its ruler, King Sa'ud, maintained friendly relations with Egypt's President Jamal 'Abd an-Nasser and opposed the British-sponsored Baghdad Pact, which he believed strengthened his traditional adversaries – the Hashemite dynasty of Iraq. Saudi Arabia's relations with Britain had deteriorated in the early 1950s over several matters concerning eastern Arabia: in 1955 the Saudi garrison was driven out of the Buraymi area by the 'army' of Abu Dhabi, commanded and supported by the British. This was the culmination of a border dispute initiated by the prospect of finding oil in the area between Saudi Arabia on one side and British-controlled Abu Dhabi and Oman on the other. The humiliating incident brought King Sa'ud even closer to Egypt. Egypt was inimical both to Britain and the Hashemite regime, and led the campaign in the Arab countries against the Baghdad Pact, endeavouring to organize a joint Arab front against the Pact, and to a lesser extent against Israel. The Saudis now appeared in the same strange situation, though they were strongly anti-communist, US-allied and reliant on American military aid. America's ambiguous position toward British interests in this area and to the Baghdad Pact enabled the Saudis to manoeuvre, while at this stage the United States' relations with Egypt still had a fluid character and Egyptian relations with the USSR were not yet entirely clear.

A defence treaty was concluded between Egypt and Saudi Arabia which theoretically placed Saudi forces under Egyptian command. The Soviets attached great importance to formal agreements between states and believed that the Egyptian–Saudi Arabian treaty might help them penetrate Saudi Arabia. When Egypt concluded the 1955 (Czechoslovakian) arms deal with the Soviets, arms were offered to Saudi Arabia. When King Sa'ud visited Iran in August 1955 he was also offered arms by the Soviet Ambassador. The Chairman of the USSR Supreme Soviet, Marshal K. E. Voroshilov congratulated King Sa'ud on the anniversary of his accession to the throne. In reply King Sa'ud said that he welcomed the offer of Soviet arms and suggested conducting talks in Cairo on arms supply as well as on establishing diplomatic relations between both countries.[7] It was clearly not Saudi Arabia's 'feudal' regime and its weak position in the Arab world which attracted the Soviets, but calculations regarding future gains. In line with their policy, the Soviet information media gave Saudi Arabia favourable coverage, presenting the presence of American military forces there as something forced upon the Saudis against their wishes, and describing Saudi policy as aimed at achieving 'real independence'. The character of the regime was completely ignored.[8] Western, mainly American, pressure and Sa'ud's fear of the penetration of communist influence that would endanger his regime did, however, prevent the establishment of Soviet–Saudi Arabian relations. In fact, it is doubtful whether such relations were ever seriously considered by King Sa'ud, who might have used the possibility as a threat against the United States and Britain over the Baghdad Pact and the Buraymi affair. At this stage the Soviets were ready to try any opportunity to enter the Arab world, and the nature

D

of the regime was immaterial as long as its policy could be presented as 'anti-colonialist' or 'anti-imperialist'. The relations that developed between the USSR and Yemen should be seen in this context, quite apart from the Soviet desire to enter the Red Sea area.

Yemen presented an opportunity for Soviet penetration. It challenged British control of Aden and of the South Arabian protectorates, which, it claimed, were part of historical Yemen. An exceedingly poor and backward country, Yemen was greatly in need of foreign assistance. Its theocratic, absolute monarchy mattered little to the Soviets in comparison to its strategic position; its hostility to the British in Aden also suited Soviet purposes. Thus both the USSR and Egypt had a common interest in supporting Yemen's struggle against the British. Egypt was ready to support anyone who would erode British positions in the Arab world (the Red Sea area in particular), and would remove them from Aden. By 1955 Egypt was already serving as a 'proxy' for Soviet policy in this area.

A 'Treaty of Friendship' between the USSR and Yemen was signed in Cairo on October 31, 1955. It renewed the old treaty of 1928 between both countries and stipulated the intention of both sides to increase trade exchanges and to establish diplomatic relations.[9] A Soviet–Yemeni commercial treaty was signed in Cairo on March 8, 1956.[10] Apparently at that time Soviet arms supplies to Yemen were also arranged.[11]

Crown Prince Muhammad al-Badr of Yemen, who visited the USSR on June 11–25, 1956, was warmly welcomed and praised by the Soviet media. During the visit, it was agreed to expand mutual trade and Soviet aid for Yemen's economic development.[12] The USSR gave Yemen a loan of about $25 million mostly to finance the construction (with Soviet help and equipment), of a port in Hudayda to serve the needs of the country instead of the British-controlled port of Aden. Construction was completed in March 1961. An airport near Sa'na built with Soviet aid was completed in 1959. Soviet military instructors trained the Yemeni army in the use of modern weapons supplied by the USSR.[13] In absolute terms, Soviet assistance to Yemen was relatively small, the equipment provided by them old and outdated, but it was sufficiently modern for a country like Yemen. For a small price the Soviets gained a foothold in a strategically important area. The port built in Hudayda far exceeded Yemen's needs, and in constructing it the Soviets more likely had in mind their own requirements. The airport near Sa'na subsequently played an important role in the Yemeni civil war. The Soviets could hardly have approved of the Yemeni regime, but what counted for them was Yemen's 'anti-imperialism' and anti-British attitude.

Soviet interest in the Arabian Peninsula countries was only peripheral at this stage. The USSR regarded the area as a Western sphere of influence which the Western powers had no intention of leaving. It was clear that anything the Soviets tried to do there would be met with strong resistance. To enter the Middle East, they needed a base, a centre from which they could move out into the whole area. Unfortunately, a base of operations would arouse Western suspicion and reaction. The Soviets preferred, therefore, to act through local forces which had identical, or at least similar goals to themselves, to find groups which, in acting in their own interests, would also serve Soviet purposes. They found such a 'proxy' in the Egypt of the mid-1950s.

Egypt then wanted to achieve hegemony in the Arab world, to expand its role and its territory. The prolonged conflict with Britain was accompanied by a strong anti-Western enmity which the Soviets nurtured. Attempts were made to persuade President Nasser that he had first of all to undermine the West's positions and presence in the area before he could effect any changes in the status quo.

The USSR had had little direct involvement in Middle East affairs. This made it easier for the Soviets to assume the pose of the disinterested outsider, of merely wishing to help the people in their just struggle against colonialism and imperialism. The USSR tried to woo Arab nationalism, by presenting it as a 'national liberation movement' to be directed against Western interests. It was prepared to support Arab unity under Egypt's leadership – provided it had an anti-Western character. Unlike Americans or West Europeans who supplied arms to Arab countries on condition that they would not be used against Israel or transferred to the Algerian FLN (which was fighting the French), the Soviets were ready to provide arms without any conditions or restrictions. It was clear to them that the recipients would eventually become dependent on their suppliers for training, replacements, ammunition, etc. The Soviets were also ready to support the Arab struggle against Israel in international forums (the UN in particular). Egypt's nationalization of the Suez Canal in July

1956 prompted Britain and France to attack Egypt at the end of October of that year. The British meant to win back their control over the Canal while the French were intent on fighting those who supported the Algerian rebellion against French rule. They were joined by Israel, which wanted to end subversive infiltration from territories controlled by Egypt, to ensure freedom of navigation for Israeli and Israel-bound ships in the Gulf of Aqaba and the Suez Canal and, if possible, to compel Egypt into recognizing its existence and signing a peace treaty. In a short time Israeli forces succeeded in controlling the Gaza Strip and the Sinai Peninsula and reached the Suez Canal.

At this point the United States intervened to save Nasser. Despite his dissatisfaction with Nasser's policy, which was more and more Soviet-oriented, Secretary of State John Foster Dulles wanted to use the occasion to show the Arab states that the United States was not pro-Israel and stood opposed to West-European colonialist policies. Aware that the British presence in the area caused Arab nationalist resentment over Britain's colonialist past, Dulles believed that Arab attitudes to America could improve. He reasoned that this hoped-for improvement would stop Soviet penetration into the Middle East and thus serve the long-term interests of the entire Western world. His policy handed to Egypt a political victory, in spite of its military defeat; it forced Israel to retreat to its former armistice lines, and Britain and France to withdraw their forces from the area. The closure of the Suez Canal and the halt of the flow of oil in the pipeline that passed through Syria made Britain dependent on American oil. The United States threatened to halt the supply if Britain would not terminate its involvement in the war immediately. The American administration, however, soon discovered that this naïve approach failed to win over the Arabs to the American side. American announcements about the need to fill the power vacuum created by the British and French departure angered Arab leaders and was used with great success in Soviet propaganda to convince the Arabs that all the United States wanted was to take the place of the former colonial powers.

The USSR threatened to intervene during the Suez War. But the threats were made on November 5, 1956, the day the ceasefire between Israel and Egypt began, which gave the Soviets a propaganda advantage without the risk of possibly having to implement their threats. The same situation was repeated a few days later on

November 10, when the Soviets threatened to send 'volunteers' if military operations against Egypt did not end. The threats were made when operations had already ceased. Thus the USSR could claim that Soviet threats prompted the withdrawal of Britain, France and Israel, whereas it actually took place in response to American pressure.

The United States hoped to win Nasser's friendship during the Suez War, but soon saw its error. It proclaimed in March 1957 the so-called 'Eisenhower Doctrine' which expressed American readiness to use military force to help any state or group of states (meaning the Baghdad Pact) 'requesting assistance against armed aggression from any country controlled by international communism'.[14] The term 'armed aggression' was given a wide interpretation, covering not only a direct attack from a communist state, but also attempts to overthrow pro-Western regimes by internal coups assisted from the outside. Countries 'controlled by international communism' included the USSR's friends in the area such as Egypt or Syria. This stiff American posture was also induced by Washington's alarm at the USSR's launching, in August 1957, of the first inter-continental missile, and of the first space-ship (Sputnik), in October. The administration had been berated for the 'missile gap' between the United States and the USSR, which made the United States into 'a second-rate' power, and it replied by undertaking a firmer policy towards the USSR and, inter alia, to stop Soviet advances in the Middle East.

In Syria, the internal situation continued unstable. The country was isolated, surrounded by 'Baghdad Pact' members, Iraq and Turkey, and by other Western-oriented countries: Lebanon, Jordan and Israel. Reports about the uncovering of an American plot to overthrow the Syrian regime drew it even closer to the USSR. In the latter part of 1957, the communists and other pro-Soviet groups grew stronger. It appeared that Syria might become the first country in the area south of Turkey (a NATO and Baghdad Pact member), to fall under Soviet influence. The fear of a communist takeover was one of the reasons for the frantic Syrian Ba'ath and nationalist appeals to Egypt to conclude a union between both countries. The union, concluded in February 1958, proclaimed the establishment of the United Arab Republic (UAR).

The USSR viewed the union with disfavour. The government of the UAR, following an Arab nationalist policy, forced the Syrian communist party to go underground and its leader to flee abroad.

The Soviets tried to use Arab nationalism and the slogans of Arab unity to serve their interests and when it suited them, offered their support. Arab plans for unity were welcomed, received with reservations, suspected or rejected – depending on the sponsors and their aims. Arab nationalism was endorsed so long as it had an anti-Western character, and was used to undermine Western positions in the area and in the Baghdad Pact countries.[15]

The Egyptian–Syrian union electrified the Arab world and caused a decline in Western power and influence in the area. It served, at least in this way, to further Soviet aims and policies. A further weakening of the Western position and of the Baghdad Pact came with the Iraqi revolution which resulted in Iraq's withdrawal from the Pact.

The Iraqi revolution of July 14, 1958, headed by General 'Abd al-Karim Qassim was welcomed in the Soviet Union as a great victory for the Arab 'national liberation movement'. Moscow recognized the new regime on July 16, and just three days later announced its decision to exchange diplomatic representatives with Iraq.[16] Close relations were initiated between both countries and agreements were concluded on trade, economic, technical and cultural cooperation.[17] Iraq withdrew officially from the Baghdad Pact on March 24, 1959, abrogated the 1955 Anglo-Iraqi agreement, and on May 30, 1959, the last British soldiers left Iraq. Iraq also abrogated the 1954–55 agreements with the United States on American aid to Iraq and the agreement based on the Eisenhower Doctrine.

The Iraqi revolution gave the USSR what it wanted – the departure of Baghdad from the Baghdad Pact. It seemed that revolution might spread throughout the whole area, which would move from the Western sphere of influence into that of the Soviets. The governments of Lebanon and Jordan asked for American aid in accordance with the Eisenhower Doctrine. British paratroopers entered Jordan and American marines landed in Lebanon. The intervention came as a warning to Iraq's new rulers not to nationalize Western oil companies and General Qassim immediately declared that he had had no such intentions. The regimes and independence of both Lebanon and Jordan were safeguarded, and Nasser received the hint that there was a limit beyond which the Western powers would not tolerate his activities. American intervention marked a change in American policy and an adoption of the earlier British position of strong opposition during the Suez War. It demonstrated to the Arab leaders the limits of Soviet readiness to come to their aid;[18] Soviet threats during the Suez War had given the Arabs the feeling that in the event of a similar situation arising, the USSR would help them. It made Nasser more confident and aggressive and encouraged his expansionist intentions. At the time of the Anglo-American intervention in Lebanon and Jordan, the Soviets threatened again, held military exercises in their southern areas, but that was all.

Anglo-American intervention revealed a weakness of the USSR in its ability to withstand the United States in the world arena, and its lack of a military arm for intervention in remote areas. This Soviet weakness, in spite of a build-up of strategic nuclear arms, not only reduced the credibility of Russian conventional deterrence ability, but even more, rendered the Soviet Union unable to neutralize American military intervention in areas important to the Soviets. In response, Soviet strategic thinking adopted a revival of the European powers' colonial approach between the two World Wars: the creation of a presence in areas vital to the USSR by the permanent stationing of Soviet naval units no matter the distances. A large Soviet navy, which would serve as a long-range military arm, had first to be built.

During the expansion of its navy, the USSR was interested in maintaining its achievements in the Middle East and widening them as much as possible. That was not at all simple in a conflict-ridden Arab world – especially with leaders like Nasser, who wanted to enjoy aid from any possible source without obligating himself. The increased persecutions of communists in Syria caused tension in USSR–UAR relations. For many years the Soviets ignored persecutions of the small and uninfluential Egyptian communists but could not remain indifferent to persecutions of members of the more powerful Syrian party. Many in the USSR opposed increasing Soviet commitments to Egypt. They were joined by those who said that the USSR ought not to provide aid to a country which pursued such policies. Even those who supported continuation of aid to Egypt could no longer dismiss the situation completely.

Soviet protests against these persecutions evoked an Egyptian reaction, which developed into an ideological dispute, with Egyptian attacks on communism and Soviet press replies that included criticisms of Egyptian leaders (but not of Nasser). Such mutual censure did not affect the actual relations between the countries. Soviet aid to Egypt continued and agreements for more aid were signed. An agreement for the building of the first stage of the Aswan High Dam was signed in December 1958. According to its terms the USSR undertook to build the dam and provide materials, equipment, specialists and a loan of 400 million roubles. In a later agreement, the Soviets obligated themselves to complete the dam. Soviet military aid continued, and the new arms and military equipment were more advanced than previous supplies.

Egypt continued to press for a union of the Arab world under its leadership. 'Revolutionary' Iraq was invited to join the UAR. The Iraqi government had no intention of relinquishing its independence by joining a union dominated by Egypt. Iraq was supported on this stand by the Iraqi Communist Party (ICP), which emerged from underground as the most highly organized political force in the country. To the Soviets, Iraq appeared as a 'progressive, anti-imperialist' state with a strong communist party whose influence over the government was growing. The Soviets could not favour Iraq's union with an anti-communist regime such as the UAR, which might suppress the ICP and force it underground again – as had happened to the Syrian CP. In the ensuing strained relations between Egypt and Iraq, the Soviets sided with Iraq, despite the difficulties such an attitude presented in their relations with Egypt; the USSR continued to consider this position a cornerstone of its mid-East policy.[19]

Officially, the ICP was illegal; actually it acted openly, directly or through 'mass organizations', trade unions and professional bodies, students' and youth organizations, in the 'republican vigilance and committees', in the ministries, etc. In early 1959, the ICP claimed some cabinet seats and the more militant members tried to seize power.

There was some likelihood for a communist success and the Soviets' temptation to support them was great. Had the ICP succeeded, the Soviets could have reached the Persian Gulf, outflanked Turkey and Iran, and menaced Western oil supplies. But the dangers were too great, success was not fully assured, it might have worsened relations with other Arab countries, ended international cooperation and perhaps led to confrontation with the Western powers. The Soviets decided to be cautious. The Iraqi communists were told to drop their demands and make peace with Qassim. Gradually the communist position deteriorated, and they were removed from leading positions as their influence declined, though they did continue to be influential in Iraqi politics. This was one of many examples where local communists were abandoned for a more promising gamble.[20]

Soviet–Iraqi relations were scarcely affected by Qassim's internal policy. The Soviet Union was interested in maintaining as large a presence in Iraq as possible, and Soviet aid – economic, technical and military – continued even though Qassim's attitude to the Iraqi communists and his other policies were not approved of by the Soviet Union.

The Soviets were far from interested in the internal policies of the countries of the area: primarily, they wanted them to pursue an 'anti-imperialist' foreign policy, remove the Western presence, create tension, and generate conflict between them and the Western powers (the United States in particular). On the other hand, the USSR was anxious to improve and strengthen their Arab relationships. The Soviets hoped that by creating a situation in which the Arabs would be dependent on Soviet aid, they would be able to prove that they were the Arabs' 'best friends', their 'friends in need', who provided support 'without strings' and 'without asking anything in return'.

These were the goals. After the Suez War it appeared that the Soviets were rather successful; they had increased their presence, established a kind of infrastructure for that presence, created a need for Soviet advisers and their aid. Actually the Soviets were still far from their target. Soviet relations in the area, even with the countries considered pro-Soviet, like Egypt and Syria (and to a lesser extent Iraq), were relatively limited, restricted to small amounts of aid and trade, whose importance lay mainly in their potential for future growth and expansion.

CHAPTER V

The Breakthrough (late 1950s–1967)

Shortly after the advent of the Khruschev era, the Soviet Union recognized the tremendous potential of the Arab countries. In addition to their vital strategic and lesser political–military importance, the Arab countries were to serve as a key for Soviet advance in the Third World countries, even opening up some national liberation and anti-imperialist movements. This policy proved very costly; it brought disappointment and caused much ambivalence in Soviet foreign policy. Doubtless the Soviets found it difficult to cooperate with non-Marxist governments (and indeed, they must have found those with no clear-cut ideology even more disturbing). At first, the Soviet Union tried to reconcile its strategy with its commitments to the communist parties in the Middle East. However, by early 1960, the interests of the local communists were overlooked for the sake of achieving greater Soviet influence in the region.

Egypt was the focus of Soviet interest – and the recipient of the most aid outside the communist bloc. In 1958, the rising United Arab Republic (pan-Arabism) led by Nasser appeared likely to sweep the Arab world. However, the decline of the pan-Arab dream with the disintegration of the UAR in 1961 and the adoption of a more aggressive 'revolutionary' stance by Egypt suited Soviet interests even more. Soviet interests were especially enhanced as Egypt struggled bitterly with 'reactionary' Arab regimes and the West and increased its dependence on aid from the USSR. Egypt became pivotal for Soviet penetration of the Red Sea and the Gulf of Aden. The reawakening of Soviet interest in the Arabian peninsula countries was inevitable after this involvement.

The increasing rift with China and the need to preserve Soviet hegemony created some contradictions in Soviet policy in the region. In spite of the substantial economic and military aid the Soviets provided Egypt, Nasser's regime imprisoned and persecuted local

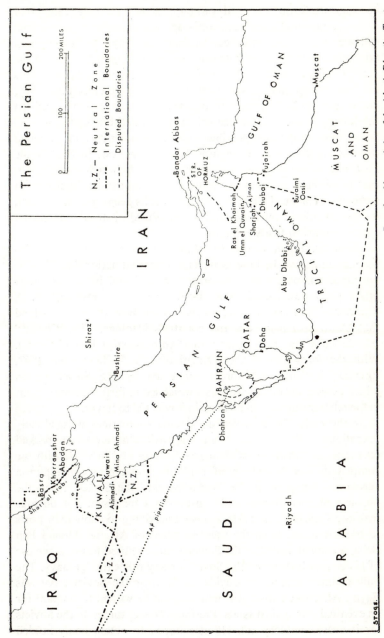

communists. Rather than acting as puppets of Soviet policy, Egyptian leaders occasionally included anti-communist and even anti-Soviet statements in their speeches. In fact, the Egyptian government attempted to manoeuvre between the Soviet Union, China and the West, hoping to 'raise the bidding' in their country's favour and thus enhance its importance. Naturally Soviet leaders resented this policy, but swallowed their pride and decided to ignore it. Egypt still led the campaign against Western-oriented colonialist attitudes, serving Soviet aims in the best possible way by directing its policy against the existing conservative regimes, Western interests in the Middle East, and by causing instability in the area. Although they did not care to admit it, this was much more important to the Soviets than a pseudo-ideological allegiance. Moreover, its geographical location, its central role in the Arab and Third World, justified – in Soviet eyes – their investments in Egypt.

Internally, Egypt turned to what it considered socialist socio-economic reforms. In June 1961, its government nationalized banks, insurance companies and larger commercial and industrial enter-prises (later described in the USSR as a 'social revolution'). A 'Charter of National Action', proclaimed on July 30, 1962, provided that 'Arab Socialism' was the country's ideology. This 'Charter' established a new ruling party, the 'Arab Socialist Union' (ASU). With the formation of the Yemeni republic in September 1962, Egyptian expeditionary forces supported by the Soviet Union joined the war against the royalists which led to further improvement in the relationship and an increase in Soviet aid to Egypt.

By the early 1960s, American Polaris submarines were already operational in the Mediterranean. The Soviets had already embarked on the rapid expansion of their naval forces and in 1964, with the completion and launching of sufficient warships to maintain a permanent presence in the Mediterranean, the Soviets faced the problem of port services and logistic bases for them. For obvious reasons, Yugoslavia and Albania were unwilling to allow their ports to become bases. Even the then president of Algeria, Ahmad Ben Bella, a staunch friend of the Soviet Union, refused to allow the use of his country's ports by the Soviet, or any other foreign navy. The only country willing to provide services for the Soviet navy was Egypt. After the Yemen war and because he wished to prepare for an eventual war against Israel, President Nasser turned to the Soviets for increased military aid. He also hoped to obtain badly needed economic aid which the West had denied. Perhaps he also hoped that by conceding to the Soviet requests, he would gain leverage over the United States, thereby forcing Saudi Arabia to stop its aid to the Yemeni royalists. Thus, the Soviets were eventually able to turn Egypt into their main military base in the region.

When Khruschev visited Egypt in May 1964, he praised its 'progressive regime' and its 'road to Socialism' and promised to increase the USSR's aid to Egypt. His promises, it seems, far exceeded what the Soviet leadership had agreed upon and on his return he was severely criticized by other Soviet leaders. Yet when he was replaced in October 1964, by the famous 'Troika' (Leonid Brezhnev as SPSU First Secretary, Alexei Kosygin, as Premier and Nikolay Podgorny, the Chairman of the Supreme Soviet), no changes were introduced in the promised aid to Egypt. Obviously, in the eyes of the Soviet leadership, Egypt's ability to serve Soviet interests justified all the aid given. Egypt had also become a transit point for Soviet arms to a number of countries – such as the Congo and Yemen. Egyptian–American relations worsened in this period; the United States refused to supply more food to Egypt and the Russians ever ready to prove that they were 'friends in need', came to Egypt's rescue.

The harsh treatment of Egyptian communists which had occasioned a flurry of mutual Soviet–Egyptian accusations ceased to be a point of friction when the Soviet leadership (following an even more pragmatic policy than Khruschev's) decided to sacrifice the interests of local communist parties to their own. In countries friendly to the USSR in the Middle East these parties were instructed to lower their profile, disband, or join the regime's ruling party. Consequently the Egyptian communist party dissolved itself (it did not represent all the communist groups in Egypt) and instructed its members to join the ASU as individuals. Many ex-communists were appointed to important positions in the information media, government and ASU administration.

Because of its relations with Egypt, the Soviet Union gradually succeeded in the late 1950s in gaining a foothold in Yemen, whose location was the main reason for Soviet interest. Royalist Yemen's 'anti-imperialist' opposition to British rule in Aden and South Arabia in general had justified some economic and technical assistance and limited military aid from the USSR. In April 1961, construction of the port of Hudayda was completed with Russian aid and the assistance of about 500 Soviet experts.[1] In September 1962 the accession of Prince Al-Bader, upon the death of his father, was marked by a message of congratulations from the Soviet Union and the promise of more Soviet aid. Soviet involvement was merely a first step in the attempt to gain an advantageous position in an area adjoining Aden and possibly even in the 'feudal' oil-producing Arab countries (which were ripe, the Soviets thought, for a revolutionary change of regime). It was consistent with the traditional Russian desire to break through to the open waters of the Indian Ocean.

The new revolutionary regime of the Yemeni Arab Republic (YAR), which came to power in September 1962, was quickly recognized by the Soviets, who also discouraged 'any foreign intervention' in Yemeni affairs.[2] Soviet assistance to Yemen was substantially expanded; the number of technical advisers alone increased from about 60 in September 1962 to 900–1,000 by June 1963. Soviet officers supervised the military academy in Ta'iz and Soviet technicians maintained the Russian-built tanks and jet fighters which were supplied to Yemen. However, arms were supplied only indirectly. Soviet–Egyptian relations continued to improve and were considered by the USSR even more important than in the past. Therefore, Egypt could and did insist on acting as the intermediary between the Soviets and Yemen, to prevent any direct military deals between the two countries. The Soviets had plans to obtain bases and services in Hudayda for their air force and navy, but such plans were temporarily shelved after the Soviet setback in Cuba.

In March 1964, President Al-Sallal signed a treaty of friendship and economic and technical cooperation which, in essence, amounted to a $39 million Soviet loan.[3] A promise of direct Soviet military support was again prevented by Egyptian pressure. Another element which thwarted Soviet efforts to establish their predominance in the region was China, which became more active in the region. In June of 1964 Sallal signed an agreement, amounting to about $28 million with the Chinese, similar to that which he had signed with the Soviets.[4] But the Chinese were in no position to compete with the Soviet Union in the supply of arms and financial assistance. Thus, despite the efforts of the CPR to expand its activity and influence in Yemen, the Soviet Union remained the primary benefactor. The Egyptians continued in their attempts to prevent direct Soviet arms supplies until 1967.

The 1967 Six Day War severely strained the Egyptian military posture. This overextension, as well as a new interest in improving relations with conservative Arab states, prompted the Egyptian suggestion in August that it and Saudi Arabia terminate their military assistance to the Yemeni republicans and royalists respectively. Egypt also ceased opposing direct Soviet–Yemeni contacts and YAR Deputy Prime Minister Juzaylan accorded Moscow rights to use the Janad airfield, near Sa'na, for direct military assistance.[5] A Soviet military mission arrived in early September and an agreement reportedly was reached for the Soviet supply of twenty-four fighter and bomber aircraft to be flown by Soviet-trained Yemenis.[6]

A new military coup on November 5 brought renewed requests for Soviet military assistance. These requests were readily received. On November 18, a consignment of Mig jet fighters arrived in Yemen,[7] a prelude to direct Soviet involvement to protect and preserve the republican regime. Arms supplies and the number of Soviet technicians grew substantially and Soviet pilots were said to have flown combat missions for the republicans.[8] However, public knowledge of even a limited Soviet involvement evoked sharp Saudi and American reactions. Saudi Arabia protested against the Russian replacement of the Egyptian presence and threatened to reconsider its own restraints on the royalists, as well as its newly-pledged financial assistance to Egypt. The Americans strongly voiced their objection to any direct Soviet involvement. Accordingly, the Soviets restricted their role. Soviet pilots were replaced by Syrians and other Arabs[9] although Soviet specialists continued to assist in training and maintenance. The USSR nevertheless watched events and retained a strong presence in the YAR because it feared that a royalist victory might not only terminate its presence in Yemen, but would also affect the future of South Yemen (which the British were leaving and where Marxist elements had succeeded in defeating the pro-Nasserite nationalist elements).

The end of the royalist siege of Sa'na brought to the fore Yemen's 'third force' which succeeded in overcoming the more radical and Marxist elements in the capital. The 'third force' Republican leaders were far more pragmatic than their predecessors; they realized they could not overcome overnight the backwardness and conservatism of the population. Their first objective was to end the civil war as a prerequisite for developing their country and moulding its heterogeneous society into a nation. They needed the cooperation and financial aid of the richer, stronger Arab countries, began to develop a far more open-minded policy vis-à-vis the West, and cultivated relations with the conservative Arab camp led by Saudi Arabia. By this time, the Marxist National Liberation Front (NLF) succeeded in establishing its predominance in Aden and South Arabia.

Another country which figured more and more prominently in Soviet policy in the Middle East was Iraq, although Soviet interests were still focused mainly on the Mediterranean and the Red Sea. After the 1958 revolution, Iraq disengaged itself from previous commitments to the West and moved closer to the Soviet Union. For a short time it even appeared likely to become the first communist state in the area. But after 1959, the Iraqi regime limited the local communist role in government and developed a more independent, less Soviet-oriented policy. Nevertheless, on the whole it remained quite friendly to the USSR and inimical to Western-oriented interests in the area. Relations with Iraq were satisfactory from the Soviet point of view.

The Ba'ath rise to power in February 1963 aroused Soviet apprehension and later, Soviet criticism. The new regime was publicly denounced for the persecution of local communists, and military aid to Iraq was decreased. But to preserve some means of pressure over the new regime, the Soviets did not stop their aid altogether; nevertheless, as the decrease occurred just as the new regime was engaged in a war against the Kurds, and as the Iraqi army deployed Soviet arms and had been trained by Soviet experts, Iraq found itself in difficulties.

Soviet–Iraqi relations improved a little following another coup led by General 'Abdul Salam 'Arif, Iraq's president, who brought the Ba'ath regime to a temporary end. The Soviets expanded their aid to Iraq. Although they gave far more aid to Egypt and Syria, it was sufficient to make their presence felt. 'Arif's policy of forging links with Egypt was encouraged by the Soviets, who nonetheless continued to be critical of his regime's persecution of communists and its continued war against the Kurds. Outwardly, both countries tried to create the impression of full cooperation and friendly relations, a posture which continued after 'Abdul Salam 'Arif's death. (Killed in an accident in April 1966, he was replaced by his brother, 'Abdul Rahman.)

Just how limited Soviet Gulf interests were in this period and how precarious its influence was is clearly seen from Soviet policy regarding Kuwait. After the proclamation of its independence in

1961, Kuwait applied for membership in the UN. When the matter (as well as Kuwait's conflict with Iraq) was brought before the Security Council in November 1961, the USSR supported Iraq's position and vetoed Kuwait's acceptance. This attitude soon changed when Egypt supported Kuwait's application to join the League of Arab Nations. The USSR's relations with Kuwait were also influenced by the strained Soviet relations with Iraq. When the incoming Ba'ath regime in Iraq continued to ignore Soviet protests over the persecution of communists, the Soviet Union decided in March 1963 to establish diplomatic relations with Kuwait. Shortly afterwards, it voted in the UN Security Council for membership status for Kuwait.

Generally speaking, the Soviets remained relatively uninterested as well as uninformed concerning Kuwait and the other Gulf Sheikhdoms. As far as the USSR was concerned – although formally independent – Kuwait remained politically dependent on Britain and economically dominated by Western oil companies. In his speech in Cairo in May 1964, Khruschev said:

> Kuwait! There is some little ruler sitting there, an Arab of course, a Muslim. He is given bribes, he lives the life of the rich, but he trades in the riches of his people. He has never had any conscience and he will not ever have one.[10]

Khruschev's words must be considered in the general context of Soviet Middle Eastern policy with its lack of understanding of the Arabs and its unrealistic appraisal of developments in their countries. In his Aswan address of May 16, 1964, the Soviet leader advised the Arabs to build their unity on a 'class basis'.[11] At that time the Soviets differentiated between conservative (termed 'reactionary') and 'progressive' (among which they had achieved a certain influence) Arab regimes. The first category included Saudi Arabia, royalist Yemen, Jordan, Kuwait and Libya; the second comprised Egypt, Syria, Iraq, Algeria and republican Yemen. The Soviet Union asked its friends in the Arab world to adopt this classification, and to struggle against the 'reactionary' Arab regimes until they achieved their downfall. However, as the Soviets did not foresee this development as imminent, they also advocated an all-Arab unity, with Egypt predominant. There was a conspicuous conflict in these two positions, but the Soviets saw them as complementary.

Despite its stated policy the USSR attempted to improve its relations with Saudi Arabia on the occasion of Faysal's coronation

E

in 1964. (An *Izvestia* correspondent, reporting on Faysal's desire to develop good relations with the Soviet Union, also mentioned 'positive measures' in the direction of social and economic reforms taken by the Saudi regime.)[12] This attempt was doomed to failure, not only because of Faysal's hostility to communism, but also because both countries were involved on different sides in the Yemen war. The Soviets also tried, unsuccessfully, to distinguish between their activity in Yemen and their relations with the other countries of the peninsula by presenting their Yemeni involvement as a function of their relations with Egypt and the struggle against British imperialism in Aden. When they realized that their efforts were to no avail, the Soviets renewed their attacks on Saudi Arabia, with Faysal becoming the symbol of 'Arab reaction' in service of imperialism.

The Gulf and the Arabian Peninsula countries attracted Soviet attention early in 1960, but the area was still not very high on the list of Soviet priorities. At the time, the USSR was more interested in destroying CENTO and other Western-oriented alliances. Although they did not conceive of the possibility of penetrating the Gulf, they welcomed and encouraged Egyptian attempts to erode the power of conservative Western-oriented rulers – Saudi Arabia's in particular. Iran, with a common border with the USSR, and reaching the Indian Ocean, was a pillar of the American 'northern tier' and formed its own special category.

In the late 1950s Iran leaned on the West for its defence. In March 1959 it signed a bilateral security pact as did the other CENTO members, Turkey and Pakistan, with the United States. The USSR protested this move, claiming that it was inconsistent with the 1921 and 1927 Soviet–Iranian treaties. Numerous notes were sent by the Soviets to this effect, some even threatening Iran. The Iranians generally ignored the Soviet notes and threats. Certain that they were containing a Soviet advance – thus serving Western interests, and those of the United States in particular – and as they considered the burden far too heavy to shoulder alone, the Iranians applied for American economic and military assistance. Above all, Iran requested substantial quantities of modern weapons to be supplied at more convenient terms than before, to enable it to defend the long Russian frontier and to counterbalance the Soviet weaponry supplied to Iraq, Syria, Egypt and Afghanistan. In reality, American foreign policy was very different from Iran's perceptions. The US was courting 'neutralist' states, which received Soviet arms and helped further Soviet interests; rather than assist their friends and allies the United States was doing its utmost to improve its relations with Egypt, leader of the pan-Arab camp and Iran's rival in the Persian Gulf. In the Cyprus conflict, the Americans drew closer to the Greek than the Turkish side, and in the Indo-Pakistani conflict the United States took a neutral position rather than support their ally, Pakistan.

This ambivalence in American policy in the Middle East was a topic which the Shah of Iran discussed with President Kennedy on his visit to the United States in 1962. The Shah used this occasion to request more arms and economic aid,[13] but was told to expect that America would reduce or stop aid to his country altogether and that Iran should fend for itself.[14]

As far as the United States was concerned, the era of containment of the Soviet Union was over. America's policy was influenced, in part, by technological developments which lessened CENTO's strategic value. By 1962, with the development of the intercontinental ballistic missile (ICBM) and nuclear-powered Polaris submarines, the importance of military bases near the Soviet border greatly diminished. American intermediate range ballistic missiles (IRBM) were withdrawn from Turkey. Although the Americans represented this gesture as a response to the Soviet withdrawal of missiles from Cuba, in reality it was made only because their presence was no longer needed.

This American disengagement from the 'northern tier' alarmed the Iranians, but they could do little to prevent it. The Shah's disappointing visit to the United States paved the way for a new Iranian policy towards the great powers, especially in view of the fact that the USSR continued to consider the countries of the 'northern tier' important because of their proximity to its own borders. Iran decided, therefore, to terminate its exclusive dependence on the United States and try to improve its relations with its northern neighbour. To strengthen their bargaining position vis-à-vis the Soviets, the Iranians claimed that the phasing out of American bases in the country came at their request. In September 1962, Iran's government pledged that it would not allow the basing of American missiles on its territory. In reality the Americans never intended to station missiles in Iran. But, as the Soviets were just as interested in improving their relations with Iran and dismantling CENTO, the Iranian pledge was widely publicized by the USSR as an important victory. According to a *Pravda* report, the Iranian government went even further and undertook to prevent its territory from becoming a tool of aggression to be wielded by America against the Soviet Union. This was hailed by *Pravda* as 'an important step towards better relations between the two neighbours'.[15] The Soviet delegation which arrived in Teheran in December 1962 signed an agreement that provided for the reopening of the land route to Iran across the Soviet Union to Western Europe. This transit agreement was particularly advantageous for the more developed northern regions of the country. For its part the Soviet Union hoped that in time it would be able to send its products via Iran to the Gulf and the Indian Ocean countries.[16] In June 1963, an economic and technical cooperation agreement was signed between the USSR and Iran. This agreement provided for several development projects and Soviet credit of 35 million roubles to Iran. Additional agreements on economic and technical cooperation were accompanied by mutual high-level visits. Chairman Brezhnev visited Iran in November 1963 and the Shah visited the USSR in June–July 1965. The most important agreement, however, was signed in January 1966. In addition to further technical assistance to Iran, it provided that the Soviets would construct a pipeline for the delivery of gas to the USSR and would purchase natural gas from Iran.

The expansion of economic relations with Iran was part of a Soviet political offensive against CENTO and against Western influence in the region. The Soviets hoped that close economic relations would influence Iran's policy, diminish its ties with the West and increase Iran's dependence on the Soviet Union. Once again they were ready (as elsewhere) to trade the interests of the local communists to further Soviet influence. Iran's Tudeh (communist) party lost Soviet support, and the activity of its members who escaped to the USSR was limited and controlled. Although Tudeh representatives continued to appear at Soviet communist party congresses where they attacked Iran's regime, the Soviets were careful to draw a distinction between themselves and the Tudeh, stipulating that the latter did not represent their views. Indeed, Soviet experts in Iran were extremely careful not to indulge in communist activity or propaganda.

The new Soviet policy effected a gradual diminution of Iran's traditional suspicions of the USSR. America's refusal to send arms to Pakistan during the Indian–Pakistani war in 1965 convinced the Iranians of two things: their new policy was justified, and they needed to diversify their sources of arms. Reports of an arms deal between Iran and the USSR were publicized in July 1966.[17] In February 1967 it became known that Iran had signed an agreement with the USSR for the purchase of $110 million worth of weaponry. The reason for this agreement was political rather than economic or military, as it fostered better relations with the USSR by decreasing Iran's dependence on the United States.[18] Indirectly it also helped Iran in its dealings with its troublesome neighbour, Iraq, whose regime in this period developed closer relations with the Soviets.

By improving relations with the Soviet Union and minimizing the danger to its northern frontier, Iran was able to turn attention south to the Gulf, where it wished to play a leading role. Ironically, in the long run, this new role was bound to conflict with the USSR's interests. At that early stage, however, Soviet policy regarding Iran continued to serve an immediate strategic need to hasten the disintegration of the 'northern tier' and bring Iran into the neutralist camp. Iran's importance as an oil producer did not yet count much in Soviet political–strategic considerations. This was consistent with the relatively low priority given by the Soviet Union to the Persian Gulf.

After the mid-1960s Soviet efforts concentrated increasingly on the Arab–Israeli conflict. The USSR endeavoured to strengthen Arab reliance on it as the main supplier of arms and military equipment. Soviet military strategists believed that the Arabs would eventually become convinced of the importance to them of the Soviet naval and military presence in the Mediterranean. Such a common interest would not only enable the USSR to outflank NATO's defences, but would gradually replace Western influence in the rest of the Arab world, especially along the strategic waterways leading to the oceans. The timing seemed admirably appropriate, as the United States had committed itself to a lengthy, costly war in Vietnam where it was utterly preoccupied. Israel was considered weak, internally divided and unwilling to go to war – particularly in view of possible Soviet intervention.

As the champions of Arab unity the Soviets determined to bring about closer cooperation between Egypt and Syria. This could only be done in relation to the Arab–Israeli conflict, but the Soviets believed that they would be able to control the situation short of war. Such a development, the Soviet Union hoped, would rally the Arabs around their flag, making them ever more dependent. Events did not develop in the expected way. The Six Day War which broke out on June 5, 1967, led to an Israeli victory that changed the entire Middle East situation.

The Six Day War was a severe blow to the prestige and influence of the Soviet Union in the Middle East.

No clear Soviet policy or conceptions existed for the Middle East – much less for the Persian Gulf – in the period covered by this chapter. The Soviets had general ideas of what they wanted: to remove the West and Western influence from the area and hopefully to replace it, to establish friendly regimes and further relations with these regimes on a strategic as well as an ideological basis. How to achieve these goals and what to do until they transpired was not entirely clear to them. Recommendations of their representatives in the Middle East were very often at odds with global considerations preoccupying the top Soviet leadership, who did not always understand the people with whom they dealt nor the true meaning of developments in the area. Often they met a new situation without thorough study or proper preparation. Frequently there were conflicting positions in the USSR on how to deal with the Middle East, reflected in contradictions within Soviet policy or analysis of events. Generally, Soviet policy in the Middle East, as elsewhere in this period, adapted to circumstances by ad hoc decisions. Observers and possibly even the Soviets themselves often encountered difficulties in understanding or analysing these decisions in their proper context. Circumstances helped entrench the Soviet presence and influence in the 'progressive' Arab countries along the Red Sea. This gain (in the long run) proved doubtful. Soviet gains in the 'northern tier' countries were even more ephemeral because the 'northern tier' remained within the framework of Western alliances, and did not join even the neutralist camps.

CHAPTER VI

Anticipating a Vacuum in the Gulf (1967–1971)

In late 1950 as the Cold War ebbed, the sharp division between the Western bloc (led by the United States) and a communist Eastern bloc (under USSR leadership) was less distinct than before.

The communist world became less monolithic and centralized especially after the Chinese People's Republic (CPR) refused satellite status and demanded parity with the Soviet Union. The disagreement between the two communist giants assumed an ideological dimension and gradually escalated into open and bitter conflict.

The Sino-Soviet conflict contributed greatly to the termination of the Cold War and the growing pragmatism in Soviet policy. Some Soviet leaders considered China as Russia's principal enemy. To avoid a potential confrontation on two fronts, the Soviets paid less attention to ideological considerations – communism or anti-communism – and more to their power interests. But, whereas the easing of international tension, as well as economic considerations, led the Western states into reducing their defence efforts, no parallel process occurred in the Soviet bloc. It continued to build up its military and strategic capabilities until around 1971 it succeeded in changing the strategic balance, hitherto in America's favour.

Even when the Soviets achieved relative parity with the United States it existed only with regard to stocks of arms and the size of standing military forces. The United States still maintained the ability to alter this balance in its own favour at will. On the other hand, the USSR would have found it very difficult to do so, as in achieving parity it had already strained its much-neglected economy. America, no longer feeling threatened by communist expansion, gradually abandoned competing with the Soviet Union for territorial allegiance and conventional military superiority. Rather, it increasingly tended to rely on the nuclear balance of fear and its second strike capability. The Americans' retreat from global obligations and the reduction of their presence in various parts of the world was in part due to their tiring of the role as world policemen. Further, they were exasperated with the Third World countries. Finally, the traumatic experience of intervention in different parts of the world in which they had little interest, notably Vietnam, contributed to the United States' withdrawal. American–Soviet relations were characterized in this period by two apparently contradictory elements – competition and cooperation. In bilateral relations and in Europe, cooperation increased, while in the Middle East, confrontation, almost Cold War, continued. In addition to the Arab–Israeli conflict, the competition in the Middle East was affected by global strategic considerations, the existence of important waterways in the region, the appearance of Polaris submarines and last, but not least, the growing importance of the Middle East oil in relation to power politics.

The dependence of Western Europe on Arab oil and the crucial importance of the Suez Canal were amply demonstrated during the 1956 Suez crisis. In reality, this crisis was caused by a shortage of tanker tonnage rather than a shortage of oil. Nonetheless, it clearly demonstrated the advantage of the Soviet Union, which was self-sufficient in oil, and the strategic–economic vulnerability of Western Europe, which depended on oil transported by sea. The West still de facto controlled most of its oil suppliers – especially those in the Persian Gulf (the source of most of the oil imported by Western Europe). The United States was still a net exporter of oil. But this advantage was to disappear by the end of the 1960s. Britain gradually relinquished its predominant position in the Gulf, the United States became a net importer of oil and OPEC began to flex its muscles. The USSR was not unaware of these developments nor their potential impact on the global balance of power – if properly exploited. Hence a major effort to strengthen its position was initiated after the serious reverses its Near Eastern policy suffered in 1967. It also began to re-evaluate its strategy there and in the Indian Ocean, preparing for a new era.

Soviet brinkmanship played no small role in contributing to the outbreak of the 1967 Six Day War. Dismissing the possibility of war as unlikely and an Arab defeat as unforeseeable, the Soviet Union calculated that an Egyptian–Syrian success (and indirectly a Soviet one) would renew the momentum of Arab nationalism and pan-Arabism, which had served it so well in the past. It had hoped that the success of this policy would lead to a clash between Arab nationalism and Western interests, particularly in the oil-producing countries, and to a greater Arab dependence on the USSR. With Soviet aid, Egypt could continue to undermine the conservative regimes of the Arabian Peninsula and the Persian Gulf, and perhaps succeed in changing their governments. Such a development would have been extremely beneficial for Soviet global strategy.

Unfortunately for the Soviets, they did not foresee the escalation of the situation and completely miscalculated the reaction of Israel and the capability of the Arabs.

During its intervention in Yemen, Egypt, pursuant to its revolutionary pan-Arabist ideology, tried to engender instability in the Persian Gulf countries and to supplant Western influence and status. Its failure to succeed (mainly because of American-backed Saudi Arabia's intervention) and the result of the June 1967 war, greatly harmed Nasser's pan-Arabism and Egypt's position in the Arab world. After the war, Egyptian policy abandoned its previous 'revolutionary' principles, as expressed in the departure of the Egyptian expeditionary forces from Yemen. Consistent with this was the rapprochement between Egypt and the conservative Arab oil-producers from whom Egypt received financial aid – especially Saudi Arabia. Thereafter Egypt concentrated its efforts to regain the territories lost in the Six Day War and rebuild its power and image in the eyes of the other Arab countries.

The Arab defeat in the Six Day War so greatly harmed the Soviet image and its influence in the Middle East that special efforts were made by the USSR to reconsolidate its position among the Arabs and whenever possible, expand it into countries previously considered peripheral. Their massive resupply of arms to Egypt and Syria and their unequivocal support of the Arab cause enabled the Soviets to expand influence in Egypt and Syria in 1968, to build a new power base in Sudan, and to implant themselves in Southern Yemen, where their aid was welcomed by the new Marxist regime. Egypt's war of attrition against Israel made it far more dependent on the Soviets – the number of Russians in the country surpassed 20,000. Never before had the Soviet involvement reached such a peak. The facilities and privileges granted them were also beyond their previous expectations. To repair the damage of the 1967 war and further expand their influence, the USSR advocated Arab unity. It also propagated in friendly Third World countries the establishment of a national front to include the local communists, hoping that eventually they would become predominant. A series of coups in 1969 in Libya, Sudan, Iraq and the Somali Republic seemed happy accidents for Soviet plans.

The Soviets strongly supported the federation formed by Egypt, Sudan and Libya in 1969/70 and encouraged Syria to join it, which she did in 1970 – unaware that its Arab nationalism was bound to clash with their interests and, indeed, it soon broke up. Soviet support of the Egyptian-led federation did not prevent them from strengthening their relations with the new Ba'ath regime of Iraq, which was friendly to the Soviet Union, notwithstanding its inimical attitude to the new federation and particularly to Egypt. Indeed, while the Soviet Middle East Arab policy was still 'Mediterranean oriented' (Egypt and Syria), the growing Soviet interest in the Indian Ocean and the Persian Gulf and the Sino-Soviet rivalry enhanced Soviet relations with Iraq, the People's Republic of Southern Yemen, the Somali Republic, and India.

The change in Egypt's policy after 1967 necessitated new Soviet tactics in the Near East and the Persian Gulf. No longer could the Soviets exploit Egyptian revolutionary pan-Arabism or act under Egyptian guise. In some instances their policy even contradicted Egypt's. It was not easy for the Soviets to accept this situation (at first they believed it was only temporary) and it took some time to adjust. The difficulty was made even greater because the Soviets' knowledge of the peoples and problems of the Red Sea and the Gulf Littoral was insufficient and often erroneous. They lacked means of direct action upon local forces, and were forced into improvization. Their resultant Near East policy was frequently hesitant and inconsistent, and even contradicted policy elsewhere.

Until about 1971, the USSR, in contrast to China, did not support subversive activities or revolutionary movements in the Gulf countries. Egypt had become more and more dependent on financial aid from these countries and was desirous of stability in the area. It even began to improve relations with Iran, the strongest country in the Gulf and vital to its security and peace. As stability was also conducive to an orderly British withdrawal, the Soviets wished – at first – to help maintain it.

In the Middle East, more than elsewhere, the Soviet leadership was uncertain as to the appropriate course of action. The Soviet Union cultivated its relations with Marxist South Yemen and 'progressive' Iraq, but wished at the same time to establish relations with the conservative oil regimes of the Gulf – above all Saudi Arabia. Iraq's relations with Iran were extremely precarious on ideological grounds and because Iran supported the Kurdish rebellion and demanded parity in the Shatt al-'Arab. While Soviet economic and military aid to Iraq increased substantially after 1968, the Soviet Union also expanded its economic relations with Iran, hoping to keep it out of Western-oriented alliances. In view of the importance of the Persian Gulf to Soviet interests, until the end of 1971 the USSR's policy there was marked by pragmatism, caution and compromise.

The Soviets were also at a disadvantage in the Gulf because they were themselves producers *and* exporters of oil. Although their oil exportation was inconsequential, they could be considered by the Gulf countries as economic rivals. More important, there was little the Soviets could buy in the Gulf countries other than oil and little they could sell (which could compete with Western-made goods) – with the exception of arms – which most of the Gulf countries preferred to buy elsewhere. There was a tradition of Western orientation in the area, British influence lingered on and American influence was growing. The Soviets, although they abstained from supporting subversion, were always suspect. The USSR had to act with extreme caution especially as it did not wish to antagonize the United States just as the West was about to leave the Gulf. Hence, despite their efforts, their achievements were very limited (with the exception of their gains in Iraq).

The abortive communist coup in Sudan made the Soviet leadership reconsider its policy in the Third World and especially in the Middle East. The expulsion of their experts from Sudan in July 1971 came as a great shock. Relations with Egypt were never the same after President Nasser's death in September 1970. There were frequent disagreements between President Sadat and his Soviet 'allies'. But it was the full support given to General Numayri by President Sadat, shortly after he had signed the treaty of cooperation and friendship with the USSR (May 1971) and despite all their generous aid to Egypt, that completely disillusioned the Soviet leadership.

Even before 1971, the Soviets had begun to question the wisdom of purchasing good-will from nations in the Third World ideologically opposed to Marxism. Ultimately the Soviet leadership decided that, considering the limited resources of the Soviet Union and in light of previous experience, they ought to be more selective. Priority was therefore to be given to Third World countries important to Soviet aspirations and ideologically close to the Soviet Union. Hence, even before their expulsion from Egypt, the Soviets were shifting their attention to the eastern part of the Arab world, especially to Ba'ath-controlled Syria, Iraq, and the environs of the Persian Gulf.

When the British left South Arabia at the end of 1967 the Soviets were taken aback. They did not understand why the West should give up so important a strategic stronghold, and were caught somewhat unprepared. The Soviets did what they could to exploit the new situation, recognizing its tremendous potential. Their activity quickly gathered momentum in South Yemen where they strove to remove the remnants of British influence and the newly established Chinese presence. Utilizing South Yemen as the centre of their activities, they also tried to build contacts with the (then) Chinese-oriented 'Popular Front for the Liberation of Oman and the Arabian Gulf' (PFLOAG), which was active in Dhufar.

In part, the Soviet attempt to erode Chinese influence in South Yemen was prompted by fear that the CPR would penetrate the entire region from Yemen and control the active, radical and revolutionary forces. On the whole the Soviets succeeded in containing the Chinese who could not compete with Soviet resources and military technology. The Chinese, as a result of policy changes gradually turned to 'respectability', discontinuing relations with revolutionary movements in the region. But the struggle between the two communist powers went on. The Soviets expanded their presence in the Indian Ocean and tried to surround China with a belt of countries friendly to the USSR, just as the West had operated against the Soviet Union.

On January 16, 1968 Britain's Prime Minister, Harold Wilson, announced that his country would maintain its military forces 'east of Suez' from Singapore to the Persian Gulf area only until the end of 1971.[1] In view of the importance of the Gulf area's assets to Western strategy, the Soviets could not accept as genuine Britain's declared intention of voluntarily giving up its predominance. In the Soviet scheme, Britain only wanted to change the form of its presence or, as stated in *Pravda*, the British merely 'leave to stay'.[2] Another distinct possibility, as the Soviets saw it, was that the Americans would replace the British in the area by way of a military pact or an alliance with the Gulf countries. The Soviets, nevertheless, began to prepare for such an eventuality by strengthening their presence in the area, so that if and when the British left, they would be able to fill the vacuum created.

The British decision to evacuate the Gulf was not only supported by the United States, but was actually encouraged by it. The Americans believed that a colonial presence in the region would encourage anti-Western sentiments and contribute to the overthrow of the conservative pro-Western regimes. In addition, this step was consistent with the policy of disengagement which America had followed since the early 1960s. The United States was convinced that Western interests and Gulf stability could be safeguarded by friendly local governments, led by Iran and Saudi Arabia, and believed that these local 'super powers' were better able to keep the Soviet Union out of the Gulf.

The first Soviet naval units reached the Arabian sea and visited the Iraqi ports of the Persian Gulf in May 1968. For the Soviets, this region was of particular significance because US nuclear submarines carrying Polaris A-3 missiles (with the range of 2,500 nautical miles) could be best deployed in this area, within range of the main Soviet industrial centres in the Ukraine and the Kuzbass basin.[3] Thereafter the Soviets maintained and gradually expanded a permanent presence in the northwestern part of the Indian Ocean. This flotilla was relatively small, but irrespective of size, its presence contributed to Soviet security, altering the status quo in the area, and accelerating political processes which influenced the global balance of power. In addition, the Soviets attempted to improve their relations with all the countries of the Arabian Peninsula and the Gulf; yet with the exception of Iraq and South Yemen (later the People's Democratic Republic of Yemen (PDRY)) their success was limited.

Soviet interest in Iraq increased after the Six Day War. Iraq's 'anti-imperialist' foreign policy, cessation of diplomatic relations with the United States, Britain and West Germany, and its anti-Western 'oil boycott', received much Soviet praise. No less pleasing to the USSR was the law passed in August 1967, granting the Iraqi National Oil Company (INOC) the right to extract oil throughout the country. This was the nearest thing to nationalization of the Western oil companies operating in Iraq. At the same time the Soviet attitude to Iraq remained lukewarm. The Soviets did not believe in the regime's durability as it depended on a small group of military officers and did little to expand its base of support. Moreover, Soviet relations with Iraq were affected to some degree by the existence of a strong communist party in Iraq. The Soviets, for instance, could not completely ignore the fact that, despite their repeated protests, the 'Arif regime continued to repress the communists.[4]

The regime of 'Abdul Rahman 'Arif was overthrown in July 1968. The coup brought to power a group of army officers, headed by General Hassan al-Bakr, considered to belong to the right wing of the Ba'ath party. In consequence, Iraq's relations with Syria (ruled by the left wing of the party) rapidly deteriorated. At first, following the rise of the new regime, the situation in Iraq remained fluid. Radical elements were strengthened, but the hard line of its military wing had not yet crystallized. To impress Iraq's population and the Arab world as a whole, al-Bakr's regime tried to appear more 'progressive' and militant than other Arab states in foreign affairs. It adopted an extreme anti-Western stance, befriended the PDRY and resumed the traditional rivalry with Egypt. The Soviets had many reservations about the character and policy of the Iraqi regime but it was the only one in the Persian Gulf they could describe as 'progressive and anti-imperialist'. In addition to its strong anti-Western policy, the al-Bakr regime did its utmost to persuade the Soviets that although it represented the right wing of the Ba'ath, it was far more friendly to Moscow than Syria. For instance, when Syria's Chief of Staff went to Peking in May 1969, Baghdad sent a military delegation headed by its Defence Minister to Moscow to request an increase in Soviet arms supplies. Finally, the Ba'ath regime, although unwilling to share power with the Iraqi communist party, stopped the persecution of local communists and allowed them limited activity.

After 1970 the Soviets paid more attention to Syria and Iraq. The importance of Iraq, as well as the PDRY, was further enhanced by the Soviet Union's growing interest in the Indian Ocean, the Indian sub-continent and because of its conflict with China. The special attention paid to Iraq began to yield dividends when it requested Soviet help in the exploitation of the north Rumayla oil fields, previously nationalized. As the date for the British withdrawal from the Gulf approached, Iraq's relative importance further increased. It strongly opposed the American-backed arrangements for the future of the Gulf as well as the existing status quo. In addition to its historical claim to Kuwait, Iraq considered itself the spearhead of revolution in the area and was dedicated to the overthrow of its conservative pro-Western regimes. The Soviet Union, which by this time had changed its attitude toward subversive activities in the Gulf, decided to put its weight behind al-Bakr's regime.

Iraq's anticipated role in the Gulf required a strengthening of its armed forces. The Soviet Union was more than willing to help with this matter, as it hoped it would make Iraq more dependent; it was quite natural at this stage that the most massive Soviet aid to Iraq was military. Here, the Soviets had a relative advantage. In other fields the USSR could not compete with the superior technology and resources of the West. Moreover, Iraq, in contrast to Egypt or Syria, could pay for all the arms purchased. The expansion of Soviet–Iraqi military cooperation received overt expression in visits by Soviet naval units to the port of Umm Qasr, previously developed with Soviet aid. It was also apparent in the growing number of Soviet experts in Iraq and of delegations travelling to and from Baghdad and Moscow.

Iraq's relations with most of the Arab countries further deteriorated when it took a strong position against the Egyptian-led federation. Its stance in relation to the struggle for power in Sudan and its special relations with Moscow completely isolated it in the Arab camp. Consequently, as Iran improved relations with the moderate Arab regimes and gave up its historic claim to Bahrayn, Iraq could not hope to mobilize Arab support for its anti-Iranian campaign in the Gulf. When Iran forcibly occupied the three strategic islands near the Straits of Hormuz at the end of 1971, the only countries willing to cooperate with Iraq were the PDRY and Libya, and their opposition was of no consequence.

Despite the growing rapprochement between the Soviet Union and Iraq, the Russians were unable to support Iraqi policy in the Gulf. They were forced to seek an approach that would enable them to take into account the conflicting factors involved in this strategically important region. The Soviet leadership, still doubting the British intention to relinquish their hegemony in the Gulf by the end of 1971, was apprehensive that by means of an alliance of Gulf countries or a military pact with the United States, American influence could replace that of the British. They were inhibited from pursuing a more aggressive policy in the region in line with their strategic needs not only because they feared Western reaction, but also because they were unwilling to endanger their relations with the Arab countries and Iran. Soviet influence in Egypt and Sudan was still strong while Egypt's relations with Saudi Arabia and Iran were rapidly improving. Finally, Soviet policy in the Gulf was influenced by their attempt to develop friendly relations with Iran and the need to exercise caution between Iran and Iraq.

Iran's perception of the future of the Gulf was very different indeed from the Soviet Union's. For the present, both countries were united in their wish to see the British leave the Gulf. With a population larger than all the other Gulf countries combined and an army which was the strongest in the region, Iran hoped to gain a predominant position in the Gulf. This by no means corresponded with the USSR's aims, but it was better than Britain or the United States remaining in the region. Moreover, the Soviets were determined to further improve relations with Iran, to diminish its suspicions of their intentions and to decrease its sympathy and dependence on the West. It was hoped to influence political relations by strengthening Soviet–Iranian economic and technical cooperation.

In April 1968, Premier Kosygin visited Iran to discuss bilateral relations and the situation in the Gulf. Evidently the Soviets wished to forestall attempts to create a Western-oriented Gulf defence organization. A few months later the Shah visited the USSR, and in March 1970 President Podgorny visited Teheran. The Shah and Podgorny met again in October of the same year on the occasion of the opening of the gas pipeline between Iran and the Soviet Union. During this period Soviet warships paid courtesy visits to Iranian as well as to Iraqi ports, and lower echelon visits were exchanged; the Soviets also became involved in several development projects in Iran.

Soviet attempts to woo Iran away from the West were unrealistic (if not naïve) in their assumption that Iran would willingly give up the West's protective umbrella just when Soviet interest in the Gulf was becoming more and more apparent. The Iranians wished to maintain friendly relations with the USSR, but unscrupulously exploited the opportunity to gain leverage in their relations with the West and to ensure Soviet neutrality in their struggle with Iraq so as not to jeopardize their plans to gradually establish a predominance in the Gulf. At this point Iran was rapidly building up its military strength so to be able to fulfil the role it wished to play in the Gulf and to challenge Iraq or any other local rival. To this end it needed American help and arms. Iran accepted Soviet aid and welcomed expressions of friendship, but simultaneously it viewed with growing apprehension the expansion of Soviet activities in the PDRY and

Iraq and the threat they posed to its aspirations in the Gulf. Iran was more than willing, therefore, to cooperate with Saudi Arabia in the preservation of the status quo in the Gulf as recommended by America.

Another factor which complicated Soviet policy in the Gulf was the growing importance of Saudi Arabia and its relations or lack of relations with this traditional, conservative regime. After the June 1967 war, the USSR recognized Saudi Arabia's new, more important role and greater influence among the Arab countries. In addition to Saudi Arabia's position in the Arab and Muslim world and its status as an oil producer, curiously enough, the Soviets believed that the Saudi market was quickly expanding and could absorb large quantities of Soviet products. Consequently, the USSR considered the establishment of diplomatic relations with Saudi Arabia even more important than before; proposals were repeatedly made to Riyadh to establish some sort of relationship, but to no avail. The Soviets did not seem to understand the depth of Saudi enmity towards communism (a pillar of Faysal's policy), and to any Soviet involvement in the area. The Saudis described the spread of Soviet influence in the region at this time as 'the communist cancer in the body of the Muslim world'. Nevertheless, led on by wishful thinking, the Soviets misinterpreted the motives for Saudi aid to Egypt, which was generally described as a 'positive step'. In reality it was aimed at 'extracting' the Egyptians from Soviet 'clutches' by making them less dependent on the USSR.

There was no immediate danger to the Soviet position in Egypt as a result of Saudi activities. During the War of Attrition with Israel, the Egyptians asked for more and more Soviet aid, which the USSR could not easily provide. Saudi financial aid enabled the Soviets to decrease their own without endangering their immediate position in Egypt, because it became still more dependent on them in the military field. Indeed, as Saudi Arabia continued fanning the flames of tension between the Arabs and Israel, Egypt's dependence on the Soviet Union increased. Soviet displeasure concerning their failure to befriend Saudi Arabia and the latter's hostility towards them occasionally erupted in the form of articles criticizing the Saudi government which appeared in the Soviet press,[5] indicating that the USSR would welcome a change in the Saudi regime. For instance, a few days after the September 1969 coup, which overthrew the king in Libya, the Soviet media reported the abortive coup against the

F

regime in Saudi Arabia which had taken place three months earlier (June 1969).[6] Such an attempt, according to the Soviets, proved 'that even the citadels of the pro-Western conservative forces in the Arab world are becoming less stable'.[7] Although this statement undoubtedly arose from frustration, for obvious reasons the Soviet Union did not wish to openly clash with the Saudi regime, and still hoped that by some miracle, changed circumstances might enable them to establish Soviet influence in the country.

The Soviets' lack of realism and misunderstanding concerning the Gulf countries in this period was reflected by their inconsistence, ambivalence and opportunism. Although at first the USSR's attitude toward Kuwait was influenced by the vagaries of their relations with Iraq, they soon discovered Kuwait's individual importance and attempted to establish better relations. The Soviets convinced themselves that sooner or later Kuwait's conservative regime would change because of the country's relative development, international situation, large immigrant population and occasional proclamations of anti-Western slogans in the Parliament and press. In an article discussing the growth of Kuwaiti workers' class consciousness, a Soviet journal claimed they had 'displayed a considerable degree of organization and resolve', establishing trade unions and striking against the oil companies. Such misconceptions generated the unfounded belief that Kuwait's 'forward movement' would eventually lead to a 'progressive' regime as in Iraq and South Yemen.[8] Meanwhile, the Soviets tried to improve relations with the existing regime and expand their trade with this increasingly rich country. But the Soviets had little to offer which could compete with Western suppliers. Moreover, because of the character of Kuwait's regime and its relations with the West, it was not even interested in Soviet arms. The only Soviet success, partly facilitated by Kuwait's fears of its neighbours, was the establishment of a large embassy in Kuwait which serves as a central 'listening point' for the entire Gulf.

The USSR was strongly opposed to plans for a Gulf defence pact or even a federation of some or all the sheikhdoms. It was convinced that the independence granted to them was nothing but a farce to justify the continued presence of Western or American hegemony.[9]

Just before Kosygin's official visit to Iran in 1968, a TASS statement accused the United States and Britain of supporting the oil companies by trying to form a military bloc in the Gulf in order to prevent the development of a 'national liberation movement', evoke mutual suspicions among Arabs, and cause conflict between Iran and the Arabs.[10] Unfortunately for the Soviets, this and the joint statement stressing the understanding and friendship existing between the USSR and Iran issued at the end of Kosygin's visit, were interpreted by some Arab countries as Soviet support for the Iranian position in the Gulf.[11] This greatly embarrassed the USSR because it did not wish to be identified with one or other side and because just at this time it was trying to re-establish its position in the Arab world following the debacle of the Six Day War.

Efforts during 1968 and 1969 to form a federation of nine sheikh-doms, the seven of the Trucial coast, (Wahhabi) Qatar and Bahrayn, were described by the USSR as intended 'to maintain the feudal regimes' against Arab 'national liberation movements'.[12] But as some Soviet friends, including Egypt and Algeria, supported the federation plans, the Soviet Union stopped its propaganda in 1969 against those involved in the proposed federation, restricting itself to attacks against 'imperialist' defence plans and 'plots'.

The federation plans resulted in renewed tension between Iran, the Gulf emirates and some Arab countries. Iran, which was opposed to the federation, had territorial claims on some of the sheikhdoms involved in the negotiations. Saudi Arabia was also opposed to the plans for similar reasons. Understandably, the Soviets preferred not to take an open stand on this matter after 1969, although they continued to denounce the 'imperialists' for their 'schemes' in the region.

After President Nasser's death in 1970 and Egypt's increasing friendship with and dependence on the financial aid of Gulf countries, Egyptian interest in maintaining stability in the Gulf grew. Inasmuch as this was the heyday of Soviet influence and presence in Egypt, the USSR could not ignore its host's policy. Moreover, Saudi Arabia and Iran gradually came to accept the necessity of a Gulf federation of a sort in order to avoid instability. Thus, although Iraq and the PDRY were doing their utmost to prevent the preservation of the status quo, the Soviet Union found itself obliged to support it, at least verbally.

The USSR's position was made even more difficult by the change in American policy in the region after 1970. The United States began to take a more active role in Arabian and Gulf politics and tried to encourage its friends to follow suit. To aid their local allies in with-standing the pressure of the USSR and its Arab friends in the Gulf region, the United States increased its aid and attempted to solve, or at least alleviate, conflicts among them. It also encouraged the countries concerned to join forces to resist the subversion and attacks of the 'progressive forces'. Consequently, Saudi Arabia agreed to temporarily overlook its differences with its smaller neighbours and to direct more resources into putting pressure on the PDRY, which supported revolutionary activities in the YAR, Oman and the Gulf. Finally, in 1971, the United States leased part of the British naval base in Bahrayn to serve the three small and obsolete warships which formed its new 'Middle East Command'. The new turn in American policy only confirmed the Soviets' earlier suspicions and caused them to increase their efforts to gain a foothold in the Gulf and to expand their aid to Iraq and the PDRY. But their policy was greatly hampered by the need not to antagonize other countries in the region with which they were trying to maintain, or develop, friendly relations.

Fear of the growing Soviet influence and activity in the PDRY, Iraq and the Indian Ocean, and their interest in the Gulf and its oil, were major factors which brought the conservative regimes of the Gulf together. This constraint, plus the gentle coercion of the West and some Arab countries, only mitigated their differences and was insufficient to bring greater harmony between the conservative rulers of the Gulf. Hence, after more than two years of negotiations it was quite evident that the seven Trucial sheikhdoms feared the domination of a more developed and populous Bahrayn, whereas Bahrayn was unwilling to join the federation unless given the position of seniority. Finally, it decided to go it alone and announced its independence in August 1971. Wahhabi Qatar, not only jealously followed Bahrayn's every move, but was influenced as well by Saudi Arabia's reluctance to approve of the federation, and thus also chose independence. Hence a mini-federation composed of six sheikhdoms, led by Abu Dhabi and Dubay (Ras al-Khayma abstained from joining for a few months) was formed in the last months of 1971.

When Bahrayn, and later Qatar, opted for independence, the Soviet Union quickly recognized the new 'states' despite its previous criticism of such 'independence' and the defence agreement which Bahrayn had signed with the British. No doubt, the USSR was disappointed by developments in Bahrayn, which it considered the most likely sheikhdom to produce a more progressive regime which would pursue friendly relations with the USSR. The early discovery of oil (though later found disappointing) helped Bahrayn to become the most advanced among the Gulf principalities, and the first to introduce welfare services, a modern system of education and a strong, politically conscious intelligentsia and proletariat. Before independence the country became the centre for political fermentation in the Gulf. As its government was relatively liberal and its society open, Bahrayn became the headquarters for a wide spectrum of progressive, nationalist and Marxist movements – not to mention strong trade unions. Notwithstanding all this, its conservative traditionalist government decided to tie its future to the West and to cooperate with Saudi Arabia and Iran (which previously had given up its historic claim to Bahrayn). The Soviets were unable to ignore the fact that most of the Arab countries granted recognition to Bahrayn. Moreover, they were faced with the necessity of competing with mainland China, which was trying to win influence in the Gulf at the expense of the USSR. But despite Soviet recognition of Bahrayn and of Qatar, which became independent shortly after, the new states refused to establish diplomatic relations with the Soviet Union.[13] The Soviets consoled themselves with the fact that Bahrayn refused to join the Gulf federation and attributed to Bahrayn 'peace-loving' intentions and the wish to establish friendly peaceful relations with other countries.[14]

When the United Arab Emirates (UAE) became independent in December 1971 (Ras al-Khayma joined the federation despite Iraqi displeasure when no oil was found in the sheikhdom), it was at first ready to allow the Soviet Union to establish an embassy and consulates in the federation. This may have been partly due to Abu Dhabi's fear of Saudi Arabia and the Iranian conquest of the three islands in the Straits of Hormuz which had belonged to members of the federation. But the strong pressure brought to bear upon the ruler of Abu Dhabi by his powerful, conservative neighbours, other Arab countries, and even some of his fellow rulers of the federation, turned the tables on the Soviets, who were thus prevented from gaining any foothold on the eastern coast of Arabia. Earlier Soviet support for the 'Popular Front for the Liberation of Oman and the Arabian Gulf' (PFLOAG) and other radical organizations was a factor which the countries of the region also could not overlook.

Soviet foreign relations are generally conducted simultaneously on two planes, occasionally contradictory, but more often complementary:

(a) inter-state relations, through diplomatic and other official contacts;

(b) relations with opposing or revolutionary groups or organizations, communist or 'national liberation movements', whose goal is the overthrow of the existing regime or a change in their policies. Such relations are usually conducted on an inter-party or 'popular' level (through the CPSU Central Committee International Section or organizations like the Soviet Afro-Asian Solidarity Committee) or by clandestine means (intelligence (KGB) or military (GRU)). Inter-party relations do exist between the CPSU and some 'progressive' Arab parties, such as the NLF of the PDRY, to a lesser degree with the Ba'ath parties of Iraq and Syria and, in the past with the ASU of Egypt. These contacts remain subordinate to the inter-state relations the countries maintain with the USSR.

The 'Dhufar Liberation Front' began its activity in the province of Dhufar (Oman) in the mid-1960s. By 1968, after the independence of South Yemen, the 'Dhufar Liberation Front' was already Marxist-dominated. It was supposed to be the spearhead of revolution and subversion for the whole Gulf and its environs: thus its change of name to PFLOAG. In reality the PDRY was the patron of the movement, if it did not actually control it; trained personnel as well as arms, chiefly from China, reached Dhufar by the way of the PDRY. The USSR was at first critical of this movement because of its belief that the region was not yet ripe for 'scientific socialism' and because of the strong ties between PFLOAG and the CPR. Nevertheless, lip-service was occasionally paid by the Soviet media to the activities and success of the movement,[15] especially as PFLOAG indicated that it did not take sides in the ideological controversy between the two communist powers and that it was ready to receive aid from the Soviet Union as well.

From 1970 onwards, when the last echoes of the 'cultural revolution' faded, Chinese policy in the region underwent a complete change. Rather than support subversive movements with a dubious future, the Chinese tried to develop amicable relationships with sovereign Third World countries, whatever their regime.[16] China began to decrease its aid to PFLOAG and grant recognition to the various sheikhdoms of the Gulf as they achieved independence, a shift which coincided with the gradual change of Soviet policy. Although the USSR hurriedly recognized the independence of the new Gulf states, it nonetheless increased its aid to PFLOAG, which by the end of 1971, was far more dependent on Soviet than Chinese aid.[17] The Soviets erroneously believed that what had happened in the PDRY would recur in the Gulf area (with PFLOAG following the pattern created by the NLF in the PDRY). Their assessment was a priori at fault because the situation in the Gulf was far from identical to that which had existed in the PDRY. The 'progressive forces' in the Gulf emirates were inconsequential, whereas the regimes were stronger, more stable, the population more traditional and loyal to the rulers than had been the case in Southern Yemen. The regimes may have been created by the British, but they were not their tools, nor did they lack support from the Arab countries or Iran. Finally, these countries were blessed with financial resources and oil which they could use for their protection. Their crucial importance to the West accounted for the West's special interest in the continued stability of the region.

Thus we may sum up:

The USSR had hoped that after the British left the Gulf they would be able to manoeuvre between rival interests in the region, and that an 'anti-imperialist' wave against the West would facilitate Soviet penetration. To accelerate this process, they strengthened their presence in nearby areas and their relations with Iraq. They envisaged developments more or less in the following sequence:

(a) The British would leave and local rulers would become completely independent.

(b) The rulers would establish relations with the USSR (diplomatic and economic), to be followed by the Soviet Union's grant of technical and then military aid to them.

(c) The new governments would try to achieve 'economic independence'; establish national oil companies assisted by Soviet technical aid and equipment; Western oil companies would be gradually phased out; close trade relations would develop with the USSR.

(d) A Soviet military presence would be established within the area, or indirectly through the expansion of Soviet presence in nearby countries (the PDRY, Somali, Iraq etc).

(e) Situations would develop in which the Soviets would be asked to help in local conflicts or otherwise exploit them. Soviet forces in the area would be able to intervene immediately should the danger of nuclear escalation be eliminated. Such intervention would have a certain 'legitimacy' and be presented as providing aid to 'legal' regimes or claimants for power.

Soviet assessment of the situation in the Gulf, in view of developments taking place in the area, proved to be extremely unrealistic
and sometimes childishly dogmatic. Saudi Arabia, with American
inspiration, closed the area off to the Soviets. The rich oil-producing
states continued their conservative pro-Western orientation and the
Soviets remained only in the Gulf's periphery. Nevertheless, traditional rulers (as well as the United States and Britain) became more
vigilant and conscious of a possible danger of Soviet penetration –
and more willing to prepare themselves for such an eventuality. To
some extent Soviet activities actually facilitated cooperation between
the conservative regimes of the Gulf, mainly between Iran and Saudi
Arabia, in preserving the status quo. It was also responsible for the
gradual change in American policy in the region between 1968 and
1971. All the same, the Soviet presence in nearby regions completely
altered the traditional balance of power in the Indian Ocean,
influencing processes underway in the relationship between oil-producing countries in the Gulf and Western consumers. On the international strategic plane, although the Soviets were kept out of the
Gulf proper, the West could no longer ignore their leverage with
regard to Gulf oil.

CHAPTER VII

'In the Direction of the Persian Gulf' (*1972–1976*)

In the 1970s the growing complexity of international relations and the interrelationships between widely scattered events reached global proportions. The bifurcation of the Cold War days between East and West grew more complicated, state decisions more ad hoc and pragmatic, which created increasingly unpredictable situations. While the United States and the USSR continued as rivals, they occasionally agreed on particular issues, in many cases opposing their own allies' positions.

Mutual deterrence made it clear to both the Americans and Russians that in the event of a full-scale nuclear war, each would suffer enormous losses, making 'superiority' or 'victory' completely irrelevant. The production of increasingly sophisticated and costly weapons and counter-weapon systems became too great a burden for Europe and even for the superpowers. Both sides concluded that a system of regular consultation was needed – not only in times of crisis and tension – but to prevent confrontations arising from erroneous appraisal of the other side's intentions and as a framework for cooperation in a number of fields, such as arms restrictions, trade, science etc. US–USSR détente was an attempt by both sides to avoid open confrontation, but it did not eliminate competition either directly or by proxy, as was the case in the Middle East. Détente was intended to prevent competition from erupting into a full-scale conflict.

The USSR's foreign relations were also influenced by the conflict with mainland China. This was partly expressed in Soviet attempts to encircle China, dominating the Suez Canal, and acquiring bases, facilities and a naval presence in the Indian Ocean. The Soviets also tried to minimize the remnants of Chinese influence in the Middle East, but this influence was of little consequence. The major power struggle in the Middle East was between the USSR and the United

States, a situation that mirrored the importance both attributed to the area and their relative influence in it. The Middle East was within the 'grey zone' in which the Powers could compete freely unlike in the zones considered the 'domain' of each superpower. The Soviet leaders' stand in regard to the Russian role in the Middle East was far from unanimous. While most major Soviet leaders accepted the need for détente in relations with the Western countries, they differed on the character and scope that should be adopted for détente. They did not agree whether its basis should be strategic parity with the United States or superiority over it, whether détente should be universal or limited to specific geographical areas and issues, excluding 'national liberation' wars, 'ideological struggle' and 'class struggle in capitalist countries' or areas like the Middle East.

Détente suited Soviet needs and provided the USSR with many advantages at minimal cost or risk. While hailing the existence of détente and acclaiming its great importance, the Soviets succeeded in expanding and consolidating their penetration and influence in several areas. Despite very little apparent consistency, in reality Soviet policy expressed itself on parallel planes (particularly in the realm of tactics). One dimension was US–USSR talks, agreements and cooperation, another was sharp competition, especially in the Middle East, where each side tried to strengthen its strategic potential at the expense of the other – irrespective of détente.

In the early 1970s, the Soviet position in the Middle East declined as the American position became stronger. With President Sadat's rise to power in 1970 Soviet relations with Egypt began to deteriorate, though this did not become immediately apparent. After July 1971, the Soviets were forced to leave Sudan and to some degree the Americans and even the Chinese replaced them. In July 1972, just at a time of Soviet policy reappraisal in relation to the Third World, Soviet military personnel and technicians were ordered out of Egypt. Generally, interest in the Third World decreased, losing ground in the Soviet scale of priorities. This did not apply, however, to the Middle Eastern and especially not to the Persian Gulf countries. Events in Sudan had served as a catalyst for the new Soviet policy, and facilitated a gradual shift of the centre of gravity of Soviet interest from the 'African Middle East' to the 'Asian Middle East' which included the major Arab oil producers. By 1970 the United States became a net oil importer rather than a net oil exporter (as in the past) and thereafter OPEC became more and more audacious. This accelerated step beyond the threshold – which might bring them into direct confrontation with most of the Arab world, the conservative regimes of the Gulf and the West. The net outcome of their heightened involvement in the Gulf was nevertheless bound to have an impact on the area's politics and on the relations of the Gulf countries with the Soviet Union.

As far as Saudi Arabia was concerned, the Soviet–Iraqi agreement only confirmed its grave suspicions concerning the Soviet aims and the need for a strong anti-communist stance. With American blessing, King Faysal strove to tighten the cordon sanitaire around the PDRY, further improving his relations with Yemen (YAR) and Oman's ruler, Sultan Qabus. They activated anti-PDRY forces on the eastern frontiers and disrupted the supply route from the PDRY to Dhufar, the Rub-al-Khali border. The British provided arms to Sultan us and brought in their own Special Air Services; Jordanian rs arrived to reorganize the Sultan's forces. Bahrayn and Qatar inated their policy with Riyadh, and pressure was brought to n Abu Dhabi not to establish any relations between the UAE e Soviet Union.[10]

Soviet–Iraqi treaty demonstrated to Kuwait even more han ever its vulnerability. Since its inception in 1961, it had the shadow of the Iraqi threat. As far as Iraq was con- Kuwait was important not only because of its fabulous oil but as an essential addition to the short strip of coast ossesses at the head of the Gulf and which is its only outlet Moreover, the Kuwaiti islands virtually control the of Iraq's three ports, including the newly Russian-built Umm Qasr.

lation of Kuwait numbers less than one million – on-citizens. The citizens are mainly a conglomeration of and merchants, and comprise only 40 per cent of the on-citizens include a very large, strong Palestinian out 18 per cent of the total Kuwaiti population) Iraqi, Omani and Yemeni immigrant communities; er Arab and large Iranian, Indian and Pakistani not without influence. Although the strong foreign Kuwait did not participate in the politics of the Kuwaiti intelligentsia, middle-class and entre- ir voices heard in the Parliament, demanding a 'progressive' policy. Kuwait tried, therefore, to

the Soviet tendency to shift the centre of gravity of their attention to the Arab countries of the extreme *Mashriq* (east) including the Persian Gulf.

Yemen (YAR) became more dependent on Saudi Arabia in the 1970s and established relations with the United States and several West European countries. Greater pressure was brought to bear on the PDRY, while British and Iranian forces were fighting the Marxist rebels in Dhufar. The Persian Gulf states concluded large-scale arms deals with the United States, Britain and France, implementation of which would alter the balance in this area even more in America's favour. The Soviets were convinced that this was part of an American 'plot' to remove them completely from the area. Soviet reaction was expressed primarily in attempts to consolidate their influence in Iraq, the PDRY, Somali, Syria and Afghanistan. An ideological sympathy became evident with the Soviet–Iraqi treaty of friendship, signed in April 1972, and accompanied by Soviet arms supplies. In retrospect, this development (considered at the time an important Soviet achievement) was generally counter-productive as it was criticized by most Arab countries friendly to the USSR, and it alarmed the West and Iraq's neighbours, driving them closer to the Americans who were willing to supply them with sophisticated weapons. It also contributed to an increased cooperation among themselves against the USSR and its local allies. Generally speaking, the years 1972 and 1973 were marked by two contradictory processes in the Gulf: America's influence grew partly because of local fear of the Soviet Union, while tension also grew between the oil pro- ducers and the Western consumers, accelerated by the 'energy crisis' in America at the end of 1972 and the beginning of 1973.

Iraq's militant Ba'ath regime was all but isolated in the Arab world. Dominated by a Sunni Arab minority it continued to conduct an intermittent and bitter war against the Kurds and its relations with Iran were increasingly tense. Its outspoken anti-Western stance, its struggle against the Western oil companies and its revolutionary ideology, propelled Iraq into opposing the *pax Americana* in the Gulf which entailed a growing supply of arms to its neighbours. Its frustrated ambitions in the region created a common denominator between Iraqi and Soviet interests and strengthened relations between the two countries. From a Soviet viewpoint, Iraq was admirably suited to further its interests in the region. It was an oil-producing Gulf country, nearly adjacent to the Soviet Union. Iraq's strained relations with its neighbours and the West made it more dependent on Soviet aid and protection and consequently more vulnerable to leverage and influence. Last but not least, Iraq's regime was 'progressive', fitting ideological as well as pragmatic requirements of the new Soviet approach to the 'Third World' countries.

A delegation, led by Iraq's 'strong man' Saddam Hussayn al-Taqriti (Deputy Secretary-General of Iraq's Ba'ath and Deputy Chairman of the Revolutionary Command Council), visited the USSR in February 1972. Shortly after the return of Saddam Hussayn, Premier Kosygin arrived in Baghdad presumably to participate in the celebration of the opening of the north Rumayla oil field, developed with Soviet assistance.[1] On April 9, 1972 a treaty of friendship and cooperation was signed between the USSR and Iraq, although the Soviets disagreed with certain aspects of Iraq's Middle Eastern policy and ignored the expression 'strategic alliance' used by the Iraqis.[2] This treaty bore some resemblance to agreements between the USSR and East European countries but went beyond treaties the Soviets had signed with other Arab countries. The military clause of the treaty (para. 9) specified mutual aid in strengthening 'defence capability'; the phrase was meant to demonstrate that the treaty was between equals, but also gave contractual authorization for stationing Soviet forces in Iraq, or for Soviet use of Iraqi sea and air bases.[3] Antonov planes were stationed in Iraq and Soviet technicians were stationed in Umm Qasr. Paragraph 10 of the treaty included an obligation not to enter into a pact for action against the other side, nor to allow use of the territory of either country for activities (military or otherwise) potentially harmful to the other.[4] It seemed significant that while Kosygin was in Iraq, a flotilla of Soviet warships visited the country's three Persian Gulf ports: Umm Qasr, Fao and Basra.[5] This visit was followed by periodic visits of naval units, possibly in line with the new agreement.

There were, however, negative repercussions to the new treaty. Even Arab countries friendly to the Soviets such as Syria, Algeria and Egypt were critical of the agreement because they considered it incompatible with Iraq's obligations to the rest of the Arab world. The agreement also caused grave apprehension in the Gulf and the West because of the substantial expansion of Soviet military and technical aid to Iraq, especially after President Bakr's visit to Moscow in September 1972[6] (when apparently another agreement to increase Soviet arms supplies to Iraq was signed). Moreover,

although the Soviets abstained from either supporting Iraq or mediating in the Iraqi–Iranian conflict, it was evident that they approved, i[f] not encouraged, the intensification of Iraq's subversive activities i[n] the Gulf. Indeed, sophisticated arms supplied to Iraq encourag[ed] them to pursue an aggressive policy towards its neighbours, and w[ere] partly responsible for the renewed Iraqi territorial demands [con]cerning Kuwait and the 'Arabization' of Khusistan.[7] Fear o[f] growing Iranian military might no doubt have somewhat co[unter] balanced the effect of Soviet activity and Iraqi threats, [but] apprehension of the Gulf countries was more than justifie[d] Iraq invaded Kuwait in March/April 1973. Hence the con[servative] regimes of the Gulf, ironically with the exception of Kuw[ait] closer together, the arms race in the region was accelera[ted] America's indirect involvement in its affairs.

The Iraqi treaty enhanced Soviet prestige, placing [Iraq] among the Soviet allies. Albeit, it was more of a f[ormalization of] existing relations and cooperation between the two c[ountries] than a long-term binding commitment and Iraq di[d not reach] the status of a Soviet satellite as some analysts predic[ted.]

The USSR expanded activities in the Iraqi oil, ele[ctric,] agricultural, machine and glass industries.[8] A[mong the] assisted development projects were the Wadi Tart[ar project,] the Mosul refinery, Baghdad–Basra oil pipeli[ne and] electric power stations, while approximately 15[00 technicians] and workers were trained by the Soviets.[9] Und[oubtedly,] to enable the Iraqis to become more indepen[dent of the West] and to encourage an aggressive oil policy [against the] West and set an example for other oil produ[cers.]

The Soviet–Iraqi agreement may, or ma[y not, be related to] the USSR's July 1972 debacle in Egypt. [The new] Soviet policy, which began to emerge [in the Gulf was] crowned by the agreement with Iraq, a[larmed] and frightened the Gulf countries in [particular who saw] the agreement a relatively exaggerat[ed threat to] Arab solidarity and to the status qu[o, which was not the] intention of the Soviets. The Soviet[s continued] their indirect involvement in the G[ulf] and to PFLOAG, but this was d[one discreetly to avoid] what they considered Western p[enetration] Soviet influence in the region. A[lthough]

navigate between the giants of the Gulf and maintain a 'neutralist' policy, which tended to be vociferously critical of the West and strongly anti-Israel.[11]

The Soviet–Iraqi treaty alarmed Kuwait even more than it did its other neighbours, forcing its rulers to strengthen their armed forces and to re-evaluate their policy. In consideration of its position and the constraints already mentioned, Kuwait continued to believe that 'buying' good-will in the Arab camp and maintaining 'neutrality' in its relations with the Powers and with Iraq, Iran and Saudi Arabia, would afford the best protection. It obdurately refused, therefore, proposals by its neighbours to join a Western-oriented defence pact and continued to criticize American policy, paying lip-service all the while to Arab nationalism and to the Palestinian cause.

The Soviets were not displeased with Kuwait's attitude and attributed it to the fact that through its booming oil industry Kuwait was entering a period of capitalism. Its anti-American stand, the Soviets claimed, was a reflection of a new process resulting from social contradictions characteristic of the capitalist era. The greater the number of workers, the sooner their class-conscious vanguard would emerge and the faster Kuwait would move to the next stage; i.e., socialism. Though they would have liked to speed up this process they had no way of doing so without damaging their much-valued relations with Kuwait's rulers. The Soviets resigned themselves, therefore, to the existing situation and tried even harder than in the past to expand their economic activity in the country. Alas, as elsewhere, they had little to offer which could compete with Japanese and Western technology, quality and price.

To some extent Kuwait's timid reaction to the Soviet–Iraqi agreement enabled the USSR to permit a certain amount of criticism of Kuwait's regime in its media. The main targets of this criticism were the country's strong economic ties with the West and its internal and external policy.[12] Another factor which incensed the Soviets in regard to Kuwait was the presence there of a large Chinese delegation; indeed, it was the centre of Chinese economic activity in the Gulf. But generally the official Soviet attitude stressed the USSR's friendship for Kuwait and a willingness, if so requested, to expand economic and military relations.

Obviously, the relatively lukewarm and meaningless relationship with Kuwait was far less important than Soviet relations with Iraq. The Soviet–Iraqi treaty of 1972 was signed, therefore, irrespective of its impact on relations with Kuwait. The shortsightedness, ambivalence and confusion of Soviet policy in the region was reflected in the fact that the Soviets did not properly foresee, analyse or evaluate the repercussions that their involvement via the treaty in the development of Iraqi ports at the head of the Gulf might have on their relations with other Gulf countries and on power politics in the region, particularly in view of the character of the Iraqi regime and its claims on Kuwait's territory.

The existence of a dichotomy in Soviet behaviour in the Gulf in this period was manifest in regard to Iran, with whom the Soviets were anxiously trying to strengthen friendly relations. Outwardly, at least, both countries continued to profess the wish to improve relations in every possible field. Certain aspects of Iranian policy, her anti-imperialistic stand and her aggressive attitude in OPEC over the pricing of oil, were in line with USSR's interests and were more than welcomed by the Soviets. But, Iran's Western-oriented policy and determination to prevent foreign interference in the Gulf after Britain's withdrawal was inimical to Soviet aspirations to establish a presence and expand influence in the region in order to achieve an important strategic advantage over its rivals.

The increase in Soviet activities in the area (which included involvement in the late 1971 Indian–Pakistani war), further attempts to dismember Pakistan, the July 1973 coup against the monarchy in Afghanistan, which led to the establishment of the pro-Soviet republic, expansion of the Soviet naval presence in the Indian Ocean and finally Soviet activity in Iraq – made Iran feel threatened by a huge nutcracker.

Consequently, Iran accelerated the substantial expansion of its armed forces and the construction of an infrastructure for them, especially in the Gulf area. In reality, it completely abandoned earlier attempts to develop a more balanced relationship between the USSR and the United States. No longer did the Shah oppose Western activity in the Gulf and its environs, although publicly he refrained from supporting such activities and declared his opposition to them. Thus Iran began to take an active role in Western plans for regional defence. For this purpose a military port and infrastructure were built at Shahbahar (on Iran's Indian Ocean coast) and Iranian warships began to participate in Western naval manoeuvres. The Iranians revitalized CENTO and strengthened their ties with its local members – Pakistan and Turkey. After 1973 they also began to improve their relations with India, both to prevent its joining Iran's enemies and to woo it from the Soviet Union.

Within the Gulf, the Soviet–Iraqi treaty was probably instrumental in the efforts which Iran made to improve its relations with Saudi Arabia, the strongest conservative Arab country in the Gulf – with whom Iran was to share the role of ensuring the region's stability. Iran also strengthened its relations with the lesser Gulf states and declared and reiterated its readiness to help them, if necessary, against internal and external enemies. The sincerity of these protestations was demonstrated by the end of 1972, when an Iranian task force was sent to Oman to fight the Marxist Dhufari rebels (PFLOAG) and indirectly combat the PDRY. Iran was aware of Soviet support for subversion in the Gulf and its involvement in Oman was a de facto declaration of its intent to stamp out such subversion and prevent even indirect Soviet intervention in the region. The military infrastructure which it began to construct on both sides of the straits of Hormuz was clearly aimed against direct Soviet intervention. On the northern side of the Gulf Iran stepped up its support to the Kurdish rebels, as Iraq was by now considered the USSR's proxy and was lending support to the 're-Arabization' of Khusistan, as well as radical revolutionary groups in the country.[13]

Although they expected some objections, the Soviets were somewhat taken aback by the strong Iranian reaction to the agreement with Iraq. They continued to profess their friendship for Iran, their readiness to expand trade relations and aid, and tried to convince Iran that their treaty with Iraq was harmless and non-aggressive.[14] Iranian communists were still allowed to operate in the USSR, and Soviet intentions of uniting the Iranian Azerbijan with the Azerbijani SSR were not completely abandoned – but on the whole, the Soviets were careful not to support the Tudeh (communist) party or any other opposition movement within Iran itself.

The Shah had no illusions as to Soviet policy and aims although he still tried to use Soviet attempts to distinguish between economic and political relations to his advantage. This was demonstrated during his visit to the USSR in October 1972, when a fifteen-year technical cooperation agreement was signed between the two countries. At the same time Iran began to cultivate relations with mainland China to counterbalance what seemed a Soviet offensive to surround it, a manoeuvre of which Iran was aware by August 1971. Iran's attempts to improve relations with India since the begin-

G

ning of 1973 and entice it away from the Soviets, together with Iran's growing cooperation with America in the region should be examined in this context and obviously did not please the USSR. Be that as it may, the Soviets did not allow their growing differences with Iran to surface and to affect their formal relations with Teheran. Moreover, following the first signs of the international energy crisis at the turn of 1972 and the beginning of 1973, Iran's role in OPEC's aggressive policy became of great importance to Soviet global strategy. Nevertheless, although the USSR agreed to substantially expand the Isfahan steel mill, the reception accorded to Premier Kosygin during his visit to Iran was relatively cool and no agreement was reached concerning the Gulf in view of the Iraqi threat to Kuwait.[15] It was at this juncture of events and following her debacle in Egypt in July 1972, when its interests became even more sharply focused on the extreme Arab *Mashriq* (East) that the Soviet Union was made again to realize the complexity of its relations with Iraq in regard to her aspirations in the Gulf.

One dimension of Soviet military aid to Iraq was the development of ports and naval facilities, which were ostensibly connected to the USSR's naval presence in the Indian Ocean. In March of 1973 Iraqi forces invaded Kuwaiti territory, threatening to continue their advance unless Kuwait would be willing to grant them some territorial concessions, which included handing over part of its coast and the islands of Warbah and Bubiyan (off the port of Umm Qasr) to Iraq.[16] As this port served Soviet warships and the incident was immediately followed by a visit to Baghdad from Admiral Gorshkov, the commander of the Soviet navy, it seemed that the whole incident was Soviet-inspired. In reality, the USSR did not approve of the irresponsible action of its somewhat unstable and impulsive ally, and the whole affair proved embarrassing. It was obvious that the Kuwait affair could easily have escalated into a serious confrontation between all the countries of the region and possibly between the Powers. Not only were most Arab countries, including Syria, opposed to the Iraqi action, but Saudi Arabia and Iran actually threatened to take action against the Iraqis and moved troops near the Kuwaiti border. Admiral Gorshkov's visit was connected to Soviet attempts to augment their presence in Iraq but was utilized to influence the Iraqis to adopt a more reasonable stance. The Soviet endeavour to convince Iraq not to force a confrontation upon her neighbours became even more apparent in the discussions held during Brezhnev's visit to the United States in June and from Soviet activity and efforts in the Gulf proper to prevent an escalation of the situation.

Generally the aggressive policy in the Gulf of the Iraqi Ba'ath regime accorded with Soviet aims in the area, although the Soviets were by now fully aware of the complexity of their relations with a country whose policy, not always dictated by reason or logic, was unpredictable and dangerous. Impulsive actions such as the invasion of Kuwait, the Soviets realized, could involve them in conflicts in which they had no interest. They endeavoured, therefore, to gain greater control over the regime or at least its decision-making apparatus. The Iraqis, on the other hand, insisted on preserving their freedom of action and were not ready to follow Soviet advice. Despite these drawbacks Iraq's Ba'ath regime remained the 'best available' tool for the Soviets, and fostering relations with it was also in line with the new concept of Soviet Third World policy. In view of their limited options in the Gulf region, the Soviets could not afford to lose the friendship of the Iraqi Ba'ath, still dedicated to the overthrow of Western-oriented conservative regimes in the region. Therefore, they acted prudently, aware of the fact that the more isolated the Iraqi Ba'athists became, the more would they become dependent on the USSR.

Unlike the Syrian Ba'ath which was also led by officers, but which was relatively broadly-based and enjoyed mass support, the Iraqi Ba'ath based its rule on the military elite and Sunni urban intellectuals. Isolated from the masses, it relied heavily on a strong and extremely unscrupulous security apparatus. Mainly because of inefficiency, economic development was slow in spite of substantial revenue from oil. Dissatisfaction was widespread in the country and in addition to their ideological dogmatism or because of it, the regime's relations with its neighbours, mainly powerful Iran, were extremely tense. To give the regime greater stability and to gain at the same time a measure of control over its policy, the Soviets constantly pressured it to broaden the base of its government (as they tried elsewhere) by including local communists. Iraq's increased dependence on the Soviets and the Ba'ath's need to please USSR was probably one of the main reasons for the establishment of 'national front' in July 1973, which included the Ba'ath party and the Iraqi communist party.

The inclusion of the communist party in the Iraqi government was only one of the signs of the growth of Soviet influence in Iraq. The USSR supplied Iraq with large quantities of sophisticated arms,[17] and an increasing number of Soviet experts were present thereafter in Iraq's military forces and in its police and secret services. At the same time steps were taken to solve the Kurdish problem and the Iraqis were encouraged and helped to improve their relations with Iran. A certain amount of success in these matters enabled the Iraqis to send three divisions into Syria in October 1973 and to participate in the war against Israel without fearing an Iranian attack or a renewed Kurdish rebellion.

During the Yom Kippur war in 1973, Soviet prestige rose sharply among the Arabs and for a short time immediately thereafter. While the United States supported Israel during the war, the Soviets unequivocally supported the Arabs and supplied sophisticated arms in great quantities to Syria, Iraq and Egypt. Soviet economy even benefited to a certain extent from this policy, because the Arab oil-producing countries, including the conservative ones, paid for the Russian arms in hard currency.[18] The Soviets encouraged OPEC's dramatic increase of the price of oil, the Arab oil boycott of the United States and the decrease in oil production – all of which caused substantial damage to the Western economy. By presenting themselves as defenders of Arab interest in general and of the Arab oil-producing states, whatever their regime, against American threats to seize the oil fields the Soviets hoped to strengthen relations with their 'friends' as well as with the conservative producing countries.

The 1973 Arab–Israeli war and its aftermath seemed to fully justify the concepts of Soviet strategy in the Indian Ocean and the Persian Gulf because although Soviet successes in the Gulf at this point were relatively limited, the rewards that the Soviets hoped to reap in the context of global rivalry were more than handsome. Soviet presence in the vicinity of the Gulf and the USSR's relations with the Arabs were utilized to accelerate processes which, irrespective of Soviet activity, were seriously eroding Western power, strategic ability and posture and causing tremendous damage to Western economy. The Soviets realized that by their oil policy OPEC, and especially OAPEC, countries were rendering a tremendous service to their global strategy, as well as contributing (albeit not substantially) to the Soviet oil industry and economy in general.[19] Hence, the Soviets now considered the conservative regimes of the

Gulf a necessary evil whose existence was justified. They convinced themselves that along with their growing wealth, eventually the Gulf regimes and their relations with the USSR were bound to change. In the meantime, there was no point in continuing to subvert such regimes or even attempting to establish a Soviet presence in the Gulf while the USSR maintained a presence in its environs and was accepted as a factor which could no longer be ignored in the region. Not only did they again try to improve relations with the Gulf principalities but they stopped their efforts to indirectly subvert the Gulf governments and encouraged their allies, Iraq and the PDRY, to follow suit.[20]

In 1973 PFLOAG and Iraq were still attempting to renew subversive activities in Oman proper as well as in areas close to the UAE. These attempts, together with other Marxist-oriented underground activities in the Gulf only resulted in increasing UAE participation in a campaign against the area's subversive forces, including the Dhufar rebels. After the 1973 Arab–Israeli war (and the blockade of Bab al-Mandab) Iran, fearing the outcome of an expansion of subversion to the environs of the Hormuz Straits, overtly strengthened its military presence and activity in Oman. Having previously restricted itself to technical aid, Iran now began to take an active role in the suppression of the rebellion, at first sending a brigade and later another of her special forces. The Shah often reiterated the possibility of intervention against any leftist revolution in Eastern Arabia.

Due to their new policy the Soviets again chose to abandon their friends, notwithstanding statements criticizing the policy of the conservatives and of support for PFLOAG which appeared in the communist Arab press and in Russian broadcasts in Arabic.[21] Indeed, in August 1974 a TASS report quoted a statement issued by 'a special congress of the Oman and Persian Gulf People's Liberation Front' held 'in the liberated territory of Dhufar' to the effect that the Front's main goal 'is to free Oman from all forms of colonial rule, and to establish a united democratic and sovereign state. The congress decided to rename the Oman and Persian Gulf People's Liberation Front the Oman People's Liberation Front'.[22]

The change in the Front's name, from PFLOAG to PFLO (Popular Front for the Liberation of Oman) reflected an apparent narrowing of its aims to Oman itself and an abandoning of efforts hitherto declared to be on behalf of the whole Gulf area. For the

Soviets, this was in line with their new attitude towards the oil-producing regimes of the Gulf and their attempts, after the Yom Kippur War, to try and expand Soviet cooperation with them: it also reflected the new relationship which began to develop in this period between the Arab oil countries and the PDRY.

The Soviets' interest in the PFLO movement has diminished in direct proportion to their decreasing subversive role in the Gulf area. They are now concentrating their efforts on establishing relations with recognized governments, irrespective of their regimes, and are soft-pedalling their connections with the PFLO. On the other hand, they wish to appear as the leaders of the communist world and of the world's 'national liberation movements', which requires giving maximum publicity to their aid to the PFLO. These two trends result in contradictory Soviet media coverage and give a true impression of the inconsistency in the Soviet position. In the meantime, the growth of Western–Iranian pressure in 1974–75 and the decline of the PDRY's support in 1975 began to tell and PFLO activity became more and more limited. (The Sultan was thus able to re-establish his authority in most of Dhufar.) This was precisely the aim of Saudi aid to and expanding relations with the PDRY which were partly intended to erode Iran's presence in Oman.

The dichotomy in Soviet policy can be explained by its short-range needs and long-range wish to see the area's existing regimes replaced by 'progressive', pro-Soviet ones. On the practical side, the PFLO is currently the only serious local element which actively works towards this goal. According to Soviet tactics of maintaining open options, although preserving priorities, it merits support. But in its role of a 'respectable' power, the USSR wishes to conduct conventional inter-state foreign policy in the Gulf. Indicative of this new policy were articles which appeared in the Soviet media commending the Gulf regimes, even their arch-enemy Saudi Arabia, for their oil policy and boycott of America.

Soviet hopes in the Middle East in general soon met with disappointment. After the 1973 war the modified situation gave rise to an American initiative and a new Middle Eastern policy, acclaimed to be more impartial in regard to the Arab–Israeli conflict and friendlier to the Arabs in general. This policy was designed to undermine the Soviet presence in the region and was particularly effective because the United States' support to, and its influence over, Israel enabled America to mediate between the Arabs and Israel, effecting

Israeli withdrawals from areas it had controlled since the 1967 war. Ironically, due to its unequivocal support of the Arabs and because it severed relations with Israel in June 1967, the USSR was barred from any such role. In addition to undermining the Soviet position in the area, America also tried, after the beginning of 1974, to exploit its new-found advantages in the region to solve problems that the 'oil weapon' created and to find a solution to the disastrous impact of OPEC's pricing policy on the West's economy by using both the carrot and the whip to recruit the support of Saudi Arabia. The Saudis and their smaller allies endeavoured to coerce the Americans into putting more pressure on Israel to return the occupied territories, by hinting that they contemplated better relations with the USSR. But neither they nor the smaller Gulf countries genuinely considered taking such a step which could have had dangerous repercussions, and they, as well as Iran, continued to turn to the United States and Western Europe for arms and industrial goods.

The Arab countries, who wished for and were now able to afford rapid economic development, preferred Western to Soviet technology, which they considered inferior. In competition with the West and no longer able to offer the Arabs obsolete arms, the latest Soviet military technology was made available to the Arab countries friendly to the USSR or able to pay.[23] The main customer of the Arab oil producers was the West and only there could the oil producers invest their petrodollars. Notwithstanding the price of oil, an atmosphere of better understanding and greater cooperation between most Arab countries and the West was created – to the detriment of the USSR. To add insult to injury, their new economic power, to which the Soviets had contributed, greatly increased the conservative regimes' influence in the Arab world. This influence was exploited after 1974, in concert with the Americans, to try to diminish the dependence of Soviet-allied countries such as Syria, Iraq, Algeria and the PDRY on the USSR. The policy, however, was not completely successful in enhancing the political independence of these countries in relation to the USSR, but was largely successful as far as Egypt was concerned. The Soviet position and influence in the Middle East thus declined and Soviet policy in the region became defensive rather than offensive.

Unrepaired during and after the 1973 war, the Soviet rift with Egypt gradually worsened because of ideological, political and financial factors. During 1974 and 1975 President Sadat began to 'desocialize' Egypt, to return to capitalism (the so-called *infitah*) and to move closer to Saudi Arabia and the United States. Egypt continued to receive arms and replacements from the Soviets, but such supplies were relatively small in comparison to the extensive shipments of more sophisticated weapon systems to Syria and Iraq, supplied at generous terms, while the USSR continuously pressed Egypt for the repayment of its enormous debts. For a time, Egypt continued to provide the Soviet fleet with naval facilities in Alexandria and Port Said, allowing the USSR to use the air base at Mersa Matruh as stipulated in the agreement between the two countries. Yet, Egypt's leadership believed that an Israeli withdrawal from Egyptian and other 'occupied' Arab territories, or indeed a solution to Egypt's grave economic problems could be effected only by the United States. As in the past, the short-lived strengthening of the Russian position in the Middle East depended on the existence of tension in the area and Arab need for political and massive military aid. Once willing to negotiate for the return of its occupied territories and convinced that it must give preference to economic development and reconstruction, Egypt found Western aid more useful. The oil countries were willing, moreover, to pay for the purchase of Western-made weaponry for the Egyptian army. Diplomatic relations were soon re-established between the United States and Egypt and, after the Israel–Syria separation agreement, between the United States and Syria. The possibility of a Soviet–Egyptian rapprochement became more remote as American influence in Egypt steadily grew.

The only unaffected Soviet strongholds in the Middle East proper, were Ba'ath-controlled Syria and Iraq, for ideological as well as practical reasons. Though the Egyptian bases and influence were important to the USSR, tactically and strategically, in the long run its foothold in Syria and Iraq was just as important (if not more so) in relationship to the Mediterranean and the Gulf. If the Soviets could no longer regulate the Arab–Israeli conflict, they hoped that through their relations with Syria, Iraq (and the PLO) they could still prevent any American-sponsored arrangements. Although they still nursed hopes of regaining lost influence in Egypt, the Soviets did their utmost to preserve their influence in Syria and strengthen it in Iraq, becoming increasingly interested as well in the Persian Gulf. By this time OPEC's power was clearly ascendant due to the 'energy crisis' and the hysteria which swept the West following OAPEC's use of the 'oil weapon'. As in the past Soviet policy in the Gulf region was of necessity ambivalent and often unrealistic. This policy evolved around Iraq, the only Gulf country where it was still relatively successful.

Whatever their policy in the region in this period the Soviets could not ignore Saudi Arabia's central position on international oil exports, nor its enormous financial power and position of leadership in the Arab world. Yet, Saudi Arabia's patriarchal 'pre-capitalist' regime cooperated with the United States (and Iran) against Soviet attempts to establish a foothold in the Gulf and against the USSR's 'progressive' allies in the area. Notwithstanding, the Soviet attitude toward Saudi Arabia remained open-minded. Despite occasional outbursts against Saudi Arabia's strong anti-Soviet policy, the Soviet media still tried to convince Riyadh that relations with the Soviet Union could prove beneficial. Once again, this demonstrated that in spite of relative familiarity with the Arabs, Soviet thinking remained removed from actuality and could not shake off the theories and preconceptions of the past.

Saudi Arabia equates atheism and communism with the very devil, and considers the USSR as a threat to the foundations of the Muslim states. Evidently, as long as the existing regime remains in power in Saudi Arabia, it is well-nigh impossible for the USSR to come to any understanding with it. But the Soviets believe that attitudes might change and in any case they do not wish to risk confrontation with the Saudis beyond their minor verbal attacks and indirect, limited aid to subversive elements in the Arabian peninsula. In most cases these attacks, too, were prompted by Saudi provocation concerning local developments.[24]

The Soviets assume, moreover, the existence of a conflict of interest between oil-producing countries (Saudi Arabia in particular) and Western oil-consuming countries, headed by the United States. They believe that their military power near this area and the political and verbal support they have given to OPEC aggravates tension and, sooner or later, it will reach the point of explosion. Then, according to Soviet reasoning, countries like Saudi Arabia will have no choice but to rely on the USSR for help. Their attitude to Riyadh oscillates therefore, between preaching to the Saudis, trying to persuade them that their interests lie with the USSR and emotional outbursts occasioned by Saudi activities, which incense the Soviets. According to the Russians, Saudi Arabia's absence of relations with the Soviet

Union was 'incompatible with the interest of both the peoples of Saudi Arabia and the other Arab countries'. Despite Saudi Arabia's 'anti-communist and anti-Soviet campaign in the Arab world and trying to undermine the friendship between the Arab countries and the Soviet Union', its best interests would lie in 'settling and maintaining relations' with the USSR.[25]

Soviet commentary on Saudi Arabia generally reached the following conclusions: (a) 'imperialism' is responsible for the bad relations between Saudi Arabia and the USSR; (b) Saudi Arabia's 'reactionary' rulers are 'willing servants of imperialism' and its allies.

The Soviet attitude towards Saudi Arabia became friendlier during and after the October 1973 war, when King Faysal became the pillar of the Arab strategy which used the 'oil weapon' against countries friendly to Israel, especially the United States. The unity of OPEC, following the increase of oil prices, also depended to a great extent on Saudi Arabia's stand. Indirectly, therefore, King Faysal rendered an important service to Soviet strategy by eroding Western economy and power.

Faysal's message of congratulations to the USSR in November 1973 on the occasion of the anniversary of the Soviet October revolution evoked intense speculation.[26] Completely taken by surprise, the Soviet leadership thoroughly debated the meaning and significance of this message and answered it by reiterating Faysal's greetings and even some of his terminology.[27] In the West rumours began circulating about the possibility of relations being established between Moscow and Riyadh.[28] It is to be assumed that these rumours originated in Riyadh to serve as leverage against the United States, but they might also have been a Soviet attempt to test Saudi reaction to such a possibility or to sow dissent between the Saudis and the West.

Any Soviet illusions about possible changes in Saudi Arabia's policy disappeared soon after the beginning of 1974. Saudi oil policy was guided by the wish to find a compromise with the West rather than forcing a confrontation with it and to exploit Western expertise and technology to the advantage of the economy of the producers. King Faysal's central role in bringing about an American-initiated Egyptian–Israeli separation of forces agreement was viewed by Moscow with disfavour. By this time the Soviets realized that they had been outmanoeuvred by the policy of Secretary of State Henry Kissinger, while Faysal's complicity in the matter became clear.

Though the Soviets had planned to organize Arab opposition to Kissinger and to sabotage the Syrian–Israeli separation of forces, Faysal acted behind the scenes to bring the Syrians to an agreement. By that time the Soviets realized that they had little to lose, that their situation was critical and required a more active and aggressive policy. From April 1974 they resumed a cautiously hostile attitude towards Saudi Arabia and occasionally attacked its regime in their broadcasts, as the centre of Arab reaction and the servant of 'American colonialism'.[29] But because of Saudi Arabia's importance they were careful not to overplay their hand so as to obviate an open confrontation with Riyadh.

Egypt's willingness to cooperate with the United States after 1974 increased the rivalry with Syria. Outwardly united, the Arab camp was far from monolithic. The influence and standing of the oil countries, even those previously considered nonentities, was increasing. Courted by all in world politics, they became the backbone of Arab power. They bankrolled the confrontation countries while walking a tightrope between the different camps in the Arab world – basically between the so-called 'progressives' and Egypt.

Evidently, the Soviet leadership now had a more realistic appraisal of the situation in Saudi Arabia and of her role in the Gulf and Arabian peninsula. The Soviets were bitterly disappointed with the collapse of the oil boycott against the West which Saudi Arabia had engineered and their inability to create an Arab 'progressive bloc' to counterbalance cooperation between the US and the 'conservative front'. Although the USSR continued to direct its policy in the Gulf region around Iraq and the PDRY it had not altogether given up hope of gaining a foothold in Saudi Arabia, especially if an opportunity arose due to new circumstances, but to no avail. On the contrary, as time passed it became more apparent that Faysal was cooperating with Secretary Kissinger to mend the United States' relations with the Arabs and to erode the remnants of Soviet influence in the region.[30]

By the end of 1974 it appeared that a situation similar to that in Egypt might develop in Syria. The Soviets, in an attempt to prevent such a process, believed for a while that a union, or alliance, between Syria and Iraq would aid their intentions. They hoped that an extremist Iraq under strong Soviet influence would lead a Syrian alliance in the direction of Soviet interests. Such a step would isolate Egypt, prevent a 'partial agreement' between Israel and Syria, and prove to the Americans and Arabs that nothing could be done in this area without Russian participation and consent. The USSR would regain the initiative and hopefully even the dominant position achieved during the October 1973 war and immediately thereafter. Despite the massive aid given to both countries, especially to Syria, nothing came of all these plans. The differences between the rival ruling Ba'ath factions – their mutual distrust – could not easily be overcome. Relations between Iraq and Syria continued to be strained and became more so with the improvement in Iraqi–Iranian relations and the end of the Kurdish revolt (see below).

At the beginning of the oil crisis in the first months of 1973, the Soviet Union was highly satisfied with Iran's pressure for a substantial increase in the price of oil. Disappointment ensued when Iran not only refused to join the Arab oil boycott of the West in October, but actually expanded its own production. Paradoxically, as a result of the rise in the price of fuel, Iran demanded a substantial increase in the price of gas exported to the Soviet Union (from 30 to 90 cents per 1,000 cubic feet). At this time, Iran's annual gas exports to the USSR surpassed 10 billion cubic meters, which meant considerable extra expenditure to the Soviet Union.[31] In view of the delicate situation in the Gulf, the Soviets offered concessions to the Iranians in areas of little importance to them or connected only with bilateral relations. For some years the Soviets had tried to improve Iranian–Egyptian relations, but when a rapprochement did occur after 1974, its outcome was quite different from Soviet expectations. The American-initiated Teheran–Cairo (or Teheran–Riyadh–Cairo) axis, emergent at the end of 1974, had a clear anti-Soviet character and was directed at diminishing the Soviet presence and role in the area as much as possible. Iran's policy was designed (a) to prevent Egypt's return to the Soviet sphere of influence, (b) to strengthen Egypt's trend away from a radical socialist and active pan-Arab policy, and (c) to prevent the Iraqi–Iranian conflict from becoming an Arab–Iranian conflict. Basically this policy was anti-Soviet, but the USSR chose to ignore this fact, and even encouraged Iraq to improve its relations with its neighbour, Iran (which deteriorated again at the beginning of 1974).

Soviet relations with both Iraq and Iran were very intricate. The Soviets were interested in improving relations with both countries but on different planes. Despite attempts to maintain a 'non-position' on the Iraqi–Iranian conflict, the USSR, consistent with its more assertive policy in the Gulf area, hinted to Iran that it was surrounded by countries friendly to the USSR and would do well to improve its own Soviet relations. The situation had immediate advantages for the Russians. Frustration with developments in the Gulf and fear of Iran's increasing strength led Iraq into large-scale purchases of Soviet weapons in exchange for oil and hard currency; this, in turn, pushed Iraq further into the Soviets' arms, and ensured Iraqi dependence on the Soviet Union.[32] On the other hand, the Soviets feared an Iraqi–Iranian war in which they might become involved. They also hoped that an improvement of relations between the two countries would enable Iraq to conduct a more active policy in the Gulf and the Arab world, that Iraq would form a 'progressive' bloc with Syria which the Soviets could exploit to halt the expansion of American influence and its attempts to mediate in the Arab–Israeli conflict without Soviet intervention.

In 1974 the war between the Iraqi regime and the Kurds was renewed and the Soviets, in contrast to their former attitude, verbally supported Iraq and criticized the Kurds. At the same time, they tried to influence Iraq to accept some of the Kurdish demands. Despite the Iraqis' dependence on Soviet aid and their fear of Iran they chose to ignore this advice. Their attitude, no doubt, was primarily the result of a general decline of Soviet influence in the Middle East but also heralded the beginning of a policy of Iraqi rapprochement with the 'moderate' Arab countries.

By the end of 1974 relations between Iraq and Saudi Arabia were already improving.[33] Iraq, which took part in the Yom Kippur War later began to participate more actively in Arab affairs, toning down its propaganda against the conservative regimes of the Gulf. By this time Saudi Arabia's power and position in the Arab world was evident and the Iraqi Ba'ath had begun to reassess the advisability of its previous Gulf policy and its utter dependence on the Soviet Union. For its part Saudi Arabia, as well as Iraq, were apprehensive of the growth of Iran's military power, and resentful over Iran's control of the Straits of Hormuz through which Arab oil, the source of their power, had to pass. Saudi Arabia was determined, therefore, to form a front, comprising Arab Gulf countries which, properly armed, would counterbalance Iran's armed forces. No longer afraid of the 'communist threat' it exploited this factor and its tremendous oil revenues to purchase vast quantities of sophisticated Western arms. It was ready to nurture a closer relationship with the Iraqi Ba'ath regime and even utilize its resources (on Egypt's advice) to return the PDRY to the Arab camp (the so-called 're-Arabization' of the PDRY). Iraqi officials appeared in Riyadh and Saudi officers were later sent to Baghdad. By the beginning of 1975 most differences were overcome and the road was paved for cooperation between the two countries as well as for a complete reversal of Iraqi relations with the Gulf principalities.[34]

The Soviets welcomed the rapprochement between Saudi Arabia and Iraq, which was compatible with their new policy in the Gulf. They hoped to gain, through Iraq, some influence in Riyadh.[35] Simultaneously, the Soviets encouraged the Iraqi regime to reach an understanding with Iran, hoping thereby to solve a conflict which proved a dangerous embarrassment in the past and a complicating factor in their policy in the Gulf. They (and some OPEC members, mainly Algeria) considered the Iraqi–Iranian rivalry as a major threat to OPEC's cooperation, if not to its continued existence. Hence, after intensive mediation, an agreement was signed between Iran and Iraq on March 6, 1975, settling all differences between the two countries.

The outcome of the Iranian–Iraqi agreement proved again how faulty Soviet analysis of the situation in the Middle East – and the Gulf in particular – was. The improvement of the relations between the two countries was immediately followed by an intensification of the long-term Iraqi–Syrian rivalry, even more embarrassing to the Soviets than the Iraqi–Iranian one. Leading to the collapse of Kurdish resistance, the agreement freed the Iraqis even further from Soviet patronage. Their dependence on the USSR support diminished, as did their need for Soviet arms and cooperation with the local communist party. It was not long before senior Iraqi leaders became involved in talks in Teheran and Riyadh concerning a Gulf defence pact – anathema for the Soviets. The Iraqis maintained their special relations with the Soviet Union, but their new freedom of action meant they were no longer coerced into coordinating their policy with the USSR and in some instances completely ignored it.[36]

The assassination of King Faysal at the end of March 1975 shook the whole world and highlighted the importance of this under-developed country to the world's economy and politics. The new ruler, King Khalid (together with Crown Prince Fahd and Prince 'Abdallah) speeded up Faysal's reforms, but on the whole his policy was quite similar to his predecessor's and Saudi Arabia's relations with the United States became even stronger. Moreover, by this time, the United States no longer even considered the use of force in the Gulf. Instead it was determined to reach a modus vivendi with the conservative producers, mainly Saudi Arabia. The Soviets were bitterly disappointed as they had hoped that if the regime did not change, at least a new era would be opened in their relations with Riyadh.[37] In reality the new government, working hand-in-hand with the United States, continued to support Dr Kissinger's policy on the Arab–Israeli conflict and was ready to go to great lengths to erode Soviet positions in the Arab world. Relations with Iraq were further fostered partly to drive a wedge between the Iraqi Ba'ath and the Soviets.[38] The 're-Arabization' of the PDRY was accelerated and aid to Oman expanded directly or indirectly through Jordan, partly in an effort to get the Iranians out of the country. Finally, a far more extreme line was forced on Saudi Arabia's smaller allies (mainly Bahrayn) in regard to the suppression of 'progressive' movements, trade unions and subversive organizations in the Gulf.[39] (Possibly in view of the impact of the Lebanese civil war the Kuwaiti authorities announced on August 29, 1976 that Parliament was disbanded, freedom of press restricted and that measures would be taken against subversive elements. In addition to the suppression of local 'progressives' these steps are aimed, it is claimed, to erode the special position of the Palestinians and limit the power of the PLO in Kuwait.)

Initiated by the United States, the second separation agreement between Egypt and Israel in September 1975 brought a further deterioration in the relations between Egypt and Syria and led to a sharp split in the Arab camp. Although the Americans have had little success with Syria, their influence in the Middle East as a whole grew, whereas the Soviets were losing ground. The very fact that they are courted by the United States contributes to the independence of action of the Ba'ath regimes of Syria and Iraq, despite their need for Soviet material and military aid. Meanwhile the oil countries gained more and more power, enjoying a central role in Arab politics, and wooed by all. Saudi Arabia is given a place of honour by the rival Arab camps, but even secondary countries like Kuwait can escape with criticizing or pressuring Egypt and Syria.

By 1972 Soviet attempts to penetrate the Gulf were stymied by the conservative Western-oriented regimes. The Soviets could not and did not wish to impose themselves on the countries of the region, perhaps because of the area's tremendous strategic importance to the

West. Also, they did not wish to alienate the countries of the region, choosing therefore the ineffective policy of using proxies to subvert the conservative regimes. Although there was a correlation between their global interests and the more limited interests of the Gulf oil producers, this was insufficient to make them acceptable to the Gulf's conservative regimes. These regimes were well aware of the danger of allowing a Soviet presence to expand into the Gulf, realizing that their true interests were with the West despite the confrontation over the price of oil and America's relations with Israel. Despite its initial lack of determination, America gradually took up the initiative and succeeded in turning the tables upon the Soviets. Gulf oil was becoming a factor which not only could prove extremely detrimental to Western interests, but could influence the balance of power in the world. The United States realized that the Soviet presence in the region was part and parcel of their global strategy. It could no longer trust its local allies to deal by themselves with Soviet pressure. In view of the lessons of the Yom Kippur War the United States began to strengthen its presence in the environs of the Gulf and to develop a base in Diego Garcia.[40] Convinced of the crucial importance of the Gulf oil at least in the coming decade, United States policy was oriented at gradually eroding Soviet influence in the entire Middle East.

The rise of Soviet prestige and influence following the Yom Kippur Was was short-lived. Thereafter, due to various circumstances and to American initiative, Soviet influence declined; their options in the Gulf and in the Middle East in general became more limited. The civil war in Lebanon demonstrates once again how difficult the Soviet situation is in the Middle East proper. It is not unlikely that the Soviets will therefore continue to strengthen their infrastructure in the Indian Ocean, for the context of their global strategy is based on their ability to exercise leverage upon Western oil routes which depend more and more on maritime transportation, whereas their oil resources still provide them with the advantage of internal lines of communication.[41]

Soviet pragmatism today is such that the USSR is interested in better relations with the Gulf countries whatever the character of their regimes. It is estimated that COMECON countries will increasingly become net oil importers within a few years. Consequently, by the 1980s the Gulf will be even more important to the USSR. The Soviets believe that sooner or later the present situation will improve in their favour and that wealth, modernization and education will cause the downfall of the existing regimes. They do realize that a long time may elapse before this eventuality, but convinced of the futility of attempting to reverse the situation at present, they are ready to temporarily accept it. Completely disillusioned with the ability of 'progressive forces' to accelerate change, the Soviets realize that although willing at times to cooperate with them these forces did so out of expediency and were not always ready to accept Soviet advice and influence. Such a situation may be frustrating, but the Soviets look to the long-term perspective, convinced that time will work to their advantage.

Iraq's importance to the USSR increased because in Soviet eyes it is their only friend in the Gulf (and due to its growing cooperation with its conservative neighbours). Yet Iraqi dependence on the USSR is gradually decreasing. The Iraqi–Iranian agreement of March 6, 1975 and later agreements with Iran and Saudi Arabia, were met with mixed Soviet feelings. The Soviet–Iraqi treaty of 1972 requires consultations before Iraq can enter into agreements, but the Iraqis failed to comply. After the Iranian–Iraqi agreement was signed (and the Kurdish revolt terminated) Iraq's rulers began to demonstrate greater independence from the USSR, disregarding the local communist party which was supposed to share in the government. By mid-1975 they even began to negotiate a Gulf defence agreement with Iran and Saudi Arabia. Yet, still feeling insecure, they do not wish to antagonize the USSR too much lest the concomitant isolation be used against them later by Iran, Syria or some other country. Indeed, because of the constant tension with Syria over ideological differences and the problem of the Euphrates waters and Lebanon, the Iraqi leadership is doing its best to maintain its special relations with the Soviets, although in the economic field it has begun to nurture relations with the West. The USSR is aware of the ambivalence of Iraq's attitude but the increasingly shaky Soviet position in the Middle East does not permit a firmer stand.

Iran's military power, hegemony in the Gulf and ability to control Arab oil led Saudi Arabia into trying to effect greater cohesion among the Arab Gulf countries so as to build a military power equal to that of Iran (Saudi arms purchases in the US in 1975/6 reached $6 billion – the second largest after Iran's – and it is planning a pipeline to Southern Arabia bypassing Hormuz). It also hopes to get Iranians out of Oman. The Shah's Middle East policy assumes that most Arab countries are inhibited from taking direct action against Iran either because they seek its friendship, fear its power, or that the Soviets would exploit the rift. Despite some benefits from a controlled Arab–Israeli conflict, Iran is apprehensive lest the escalation of this conflict affect the Gulf. The Iranians have no illusions where the USSR would stand in the case of an Arab–Iranian conflict, nor about Soviet intentions and ability to exploit the situation. Notwithstanding, they still promote trade relations with the Soviets, hoping to prevent such an eventuality and in order to maintain some options in their complicated relationship with the US.

The Soviets adopted an attitude similar to Iran's since they generally distinguish between trade and politics. Though aware that Iranian policy is clearly directed against their presence in the Middle East they can do little about it at present. But in so far as Iran's oil policy leads her to constantly press OPEC to raise oil prices it serves Soviet interests. Indeed, the Shah's grand ambitions contribute to the same purpose, generating constant tension in the area and leading to some friction with America.

For the time being, due to its regional and international importance, Saudi Arabia remained a focus of Soviet interest. Despite Saudi co-operation with the United States and hostility to them, the Soviets exercise great restraint, believing in the inevitable clash between Saudi Arabia and the Western oil-importing countries, which will coerce the Saudis into asking them for aid. The Soviets believe, moreover, that the present regime in Riyadh is bound to be affected by the rapid development and internal changes experienced by the Arab countries in general, and the Gulf countries in particular. Perhaps undergoing at least a 'white revolution' it will be taken over by the newly emergent nationalistic bourgeoisie. But the Soviets' real hope is that the Saudi regime be overthrown by a military revolution likely to adopt a Ba'ath-type ideology and move closer to the USSR, causing a chain reaction in Eastern Arabia. The status of the new revolutionary regimes could not then be exploited by Western intervention without due consideration being given to local or Soviet reaction. King Faysal's assassination confirmed, if proof was needed, how vulnerable and dependent on personalities the area's regimes are and how a single event could lead to a major upheaval. This only reinforces the Soviet's premise that it is wise to bide their time and not to exert pressures which could provoke unfavourable reaction.

CHAPTER VIII

South Yemen – The Cuba of the Middle East[1]

The geographical position of southern Arabia has long given it strategic importance. Close to the world's major oil sources, it overlooks both the Indian Ocean and the Red Sea, whose southern entrance it directly controls. For years the port of Aden served Britain as a station to the Persian Gulf, India and East Africa and now attracts the Soviets for the same reasons.

A National Liberation Front (NLF) motivated by socialist ideology was established in Aden in 1963, dedicated from its inception to armed rebellion against the British and their 'lackeys', the ruling classes. By providing inspiring leadership the NLF General Command soon managed to transform an ordinary tribal uprising in the Radfan mountains into the nucleus of a popular war of liberation. With Egyptian and Yemeni Republican help, this rebellion gradually expanded into all the British protectorates, despite the frantic efforts of the South Arabian federal government to crush it.

The British handed over the government of South Arabia to the NLF and on November 30, 1967 an independent unitary state was proclaimed under the name of the People's Republic of South Yemen (PRSY).

The brief history of South Yemen is highlighted by an increasingly radical policy line accompanied by endemic financial crisis and a ruthless struggle for power within the NLF. With their rival organization's power broken before independence, it seemed that nothing could curb the revolutionary Marxist zeal of the NLF leadership. Overconfident from their success on the battlefield, a majority of the young radicals wanted an immediate upheaval of the country's socio-economic structure, regardless of conditions and consequences. In accordance with the NLF's ideology, they considered themselves bound to take an active role in the struggle against Israel and to support 'world revolution'. Surprisingly, it was the

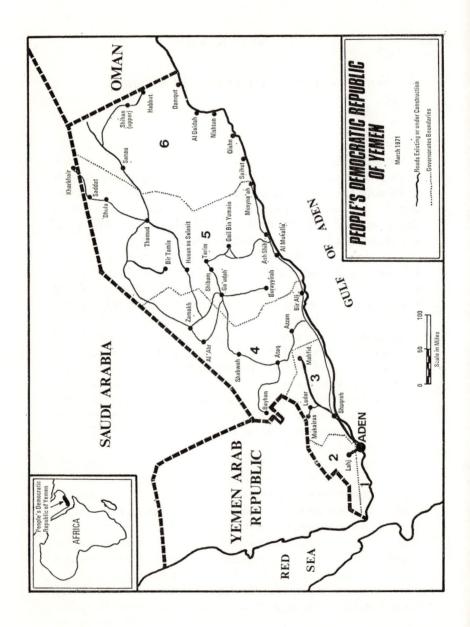

NLF's moderate wing, led by Qahtan ash-Sha'abi rather than the extremists, which formed the government of Aden at the end of 1967.

Although ideologically Marxists as well, ash-Sha'abi and his supporters, with no mineral resources in their country and limited scope for agricultural development, advocated a more realistic and pragmatic policy than did their adversaries. South Yemen's service economy suffered a disastrous blow from the closure of the Suez Canal and the departure of the British in 1967. Government revenues declined and in 1968 the British stopped their small subsidy when requested to withdraw their military advisers. Communist countries' aid was still very limited. Despite the NLF's ambivalent attitude towards 'Arab bourgeois chauvinism', ash-Sha'abi turned to 'progressive' Arab countries for help. To avoid antagonizing these countries and because the PRSY's government was convinced that the backward population was not ready for far-reaching socio-economic reforms, it was considered prudent to delay, or at least limit, such measures. Moreover, ash-Sha'abi feared that indiscriminate implementation of reforms at that stage would completely unsettle the tottering economy and exacerbate the divisive factors in the country. He tried to strike a balance between capitalist laissez faire and socialist etatism, careful not to harm the country's economy by unrealistic dogmatism. Some consideration was given to Aden's middle-class and the administrative economic framework left by the former government continued to function on the whole.

The hesitant reforms and pragmatic policy of the government were strongly criticized by the NLF militants. Their discontent and power were manifested at the party's congress held in Zinjibar in March 1968. Despite ash-Sha'abi's opposition, the congress adopted a most radical socialist programme to bring about an immediate overturn of the socio-economic structure of the country and a re-orientation of its foreign policy. The government was to draw its power from a coalition of intellectuals, poor farmers, workers and soldiers and lead the country towards 'scientific socialism' through a process of continuous revolution. The army was to be reorganized and politicized and a people's militia established to protect the revolution against 'opportunistic elements' and help bring it into the countryside.

Immediately upon its establishment, the PRSY was recognized by the USSR.[2] Very little Soviet aid actually materialized in addition to verbal support. On unofficial occasions, criticism was voiced and young PRSY leaders were described as hot-headed, unreliable, dogmatic and over-sanguine regarding reforms, nationalizations and attempts to transform an undeveloped country with a nomad-tribal society into scientific socialism. Worst of all from the Soviet point of view were its close relations with the CPR.

At first the involvement of the CPR in South Yemen was indirect and mainly within the framework of its revolutionary anti-colonialist policy. Together with the NLF it began in 1968 to support the rebellion in Dhufar, involving itself only with small quantities of light arms and training of guerrillas. The Soviets, however, feared the possible expansion of such involvement. This, in addition to the PRSY's strategic importance, encouraged them to try and maintain their own presence there. But in the remote corner of the Arabian Peninsula Soviet efforts and aid were on a limited scale compared to other Arab countries. Small quantities of obsolete military equipment were given by the Soviets as grants, or an approximation thereof, as the PRSY could hardly have afforded to pay for them. Soviet economic aid was still too limited to solve the country's economic difficulties.

It was in such a situation, in great need of foreign aid, that President ash-Sha'abi visited the USSR in February 1969. During the visit agreements on economic and technical cooperation and air communications were signed.[3] This last item was important for the Soviets as it gave them landing possibilities en route to the Indian Ocean and adjacent countries. The Soviets were nevertheless suspicious of ash-Sha'abi's pragmatic policy and relations with the CPR. Though he acted against the extreme leftists, he allowed the Chinese to open their largest diplomatic mission in the Middle East in Aden, and to conduct an extensive economic survey of the country.[4]

The visit coincided with differences in the ruling NLF party between President ash-Sha'abi and more militant leftists, led by the party's ideologist, 'Abdul Fattah Isma'il, and by Salim Ruba'i 'Ali, who had gradually increased their power in the capital and the provinces. Consequently, President ash-Sha'abi was forced by the radicals to resign in June 1969, and was replaced by a Presidential Council headed by Ruba'i 'Ali. It included NLF Secretary-General 'Abdul Fattah Isma'il, for a time the country's 'strong man' and Prime Minister Muhammad 'Ali Haytham who represented more moderate 'tribalist' elements in the party.

The party's hard-core ideologists, especially 'Abdul Fattah Isma'il and the small North Yemeni group in the NLF, were critical of the tribal allegiances which they felt were detrimental to national integration. Dedicated to unification of both Yemens on their own terms, they were partly responsible for the growing tension between the two countries. Instrumental in fostering relations with the Soviet Union and expanding Soviet aid, Isma'il and his supporters were described as the pro-Soviet faction in the NLF. President Salim Ruba'i, at this period still in Isma'il's shadow, represented another group of radicals made up solely of South Yemenis. This faction was even more militant concerning acceleration of the pace of socio-economic reforms and reorganization and politicization of the armed forces. In disagreement with Isma'il over relations with North Yemen and the 'progressive' Arab countries, this group began to foster relations with the CPR. As rivalry was generally more personal than ideological, both factions were composed of elements of varying opinions.

In foreign relations, the new regime unequivocally placed itself in the revolutionary socialist camp and made determined efforts to develop its ties with the communist countries. Relations with the West, on the other hand, deteriorated sharply. Not only was 'world revolution' preached, but Aden, an important centre of revolutionary movements, intensified its subversion of 'reactionary' governments. Devoted to Marxist–Leninist ideology and hypnotized by dogmatic interpretations of socialism, the NLF radicals completely ignored South Yemen's economic realities and were determined to transform their country's backward capitalist (and to a great extent pre-capitalist) economy into a socialist one in the shortest possible time. Foreign assets and several branches of the PRSY economy were immediately nationalized and in 1970 agrarian reform was introduced and implemented. Still dissatisfied with the pace of reform, the 'ultras' initiated 'revolutions' of poor peasants, fishermen and workers against employers and tried to enforce collectivization in different sectors of the economy.

By 1970, it appeared that the NLF's radical reforms and dogmatic policy were leading the country towards bankruptcy and isolation. Aden's service economy stagnated further, unemployment grew constantly. Even in the countryside, the agrarian reforms and 'peasant revolutions' bred chaos, which damaged agricultural production.

From the ideological, military and economic points of view and because most Arab countries were still lukewarm toward the regime, it was important to the NLF radicals to win the support of the Soviet Union. However, the Soviet Union was in no hurry to expand its aid to the PRSY, nor to commit itself to such aid in the near future, preferring to wait and see the direction the PRSY regime would take.

The PRSY leaders' militancy and conflicts with their neighbours made the Russians unwilling to commit themselves there as they did in Egypt. Any increased Soviet aid would harden the PRSY leaders' positions even further, and lead to a war between them and their neighbours, with Saudi Arabia in particular. That, the Soviets feared, might involve them in a Middle East conflict and strain relations with the US when there were chances for improvement.

Saudi Arabia, seriously worried about the radicalization of Aden's regime and policy, began to take steps to overthrow the NLF government in Aden.[5] Tension between the two Yemens increased when Isma'il's group, which became influential in the South with the help of radical political refugees from the North, began to subvert the YAR's government, now steadily moving towards moderation and better relations with Saudi Arabia. Moreover, elements inimical to the NLF who found refuge in the YAR constantly reinforced their guerrilla warfare against the PRSY (after November 1970 'The People's Democratic Republic of the Yemen' – PDRY), causing further financial and political difficulties.

The NLF radicals were divided ideologically into two main camps: the first, Maoist in orientation and pro-Chinese, was led by President Ruba'i; the second, less radical, Marxist and pro-Soviet, was led by 'Abdul Fattah Isma'il. In fact, although seemingly motivated by ideology, the respective connections of the two leaders with the CPR and the USSR were to a large extent a matter of tactics and the result of personal rivalry enhanced by differences in origin, background and outlook. Each believed in the PDRY's brand of 'scientific socialism', and even Isma'il did not want the PDRY to become a Soviet client. Disregarding Soviet displeasure, he pressed for the implementation of the Zinjibar socio-economic reforms and undermined the position of 'Abdallah Badhib, the leader of the small pro-Moscow communist party. Salim Ruba'i 'Ali, on the other hand, rejected China's doctrine of possible cooperation with the petit bourgeoisie, and was critical of the CPR's policy of respectability and betrayal of 'world revolution'.[6]

The Soviets showed particular interest in the development of inter-party cooperation between the CPSU and the NLF which they eventually intended turning into a communist party in all but name, under Soviet leadership and guidance. The Soviets tried to penetrate the NLF and gain influence over it by assistance in its organization, preparation of cadres, organization of party courses and by inviting its leaders to visit the Soviet Union. An agreement was reached during Isma'il's Soviet visit in May 1970.[7] An NLF Party School was established on the Soviet pattern, and included Soviet lecturers; calls to strengthen inter-party cooperation appeared afterwards in most joint PDRY–USSR statements.

In July 1971, immediately after Isma'il's return from Moscow (and probably with the Russians' blessing) the NLF General Command Executive Council and the Cabinet were reshuffled. Prime Minister Haytham (who had purged his government of its more radical elements and had expressed willingness to accept aid from non-communist sources) and his supporters were left out of both bodies. Power rested thereafter solely in the hands of Isma'il, the Party General Secretary, and President Ruba'i. Ruba'i immediately accelerated the pace of socio-economic reforms and the process of politicizing the armed forces. Greater progress was achieved in collectivization and the development of the people's militia. By 1973 all private enterprise of consequence in Aden and other urban centres was nationalized. In the meantime 'Abdul Fattah reorganized and gradually expanded the NLF, reinforcing it by developing various militant Marxist organizations. Those who urged the necessity of improving relations with the West, in view of the communist countries' inability to solve the PDRY's grave economic problems, were persecuted.

Tribal allegiances are still exceedingly important in the PDRY. In a climate of endless personal rivalries, tribal support, especially when accompanied by influence in the army, is crucial. Manoeuvring within such a set-up, Isma'il was at a disadvantage because of his North Yemeni origin. By the second half of 1972 it was evident that Ruba'i was victorious over Isma'il. Always pragmatic in its relations with overseas allies, Moscow quickly made overtures to the victor. Ruba'i was willing to take advantage of this and in November 1972 was warmly received in Moscow.[8]

The USSR, despite the closure of the Suez Canal, was trying to acquire new military facilities in the countries of the Red Sea and the Gulf of Aden in addition to those it already had in Yemen. The proximity of the area to the oil-rich Persian Gulf as well as the continuing East–West rivalry were no doubt major considerations. Subsequently, the Soviet Union although still dissatisfied with NLF policy, and cautious about committing itself to defend so irresponsible and unpredictable an ally, began to increase its commitments to South Yemen.

Sino-Soviet rivalry was not the sole factor contributing to the NLF's advantage. The YAR's gradual movement toward the West, the approaching British withdrawal from the Persian Gulf, exaggerated reports (originating in Aden) of 'Saudi–CIA–British plots' against the PDRY and even the ineffective pressures on the PDRY border made Moscow reconsider its assessment of the PDRY, now considering it a possible asset rather than a liability. The USSR (along with its East European allies) began to increase aid to Aden's Marxist regime in the form of low interest loans plus economic and military aid.

External pressure and the difficult economic situation made Soviet aid, small as it was, essential to the survival of the NLF regime. The Soviets were not overpopular in the PDRY, but the NLF militants, aware of the Soviet Union's technical and economic superiority over the CPR, showed surprising flexibility in their relations with the USSR. Ideologically justified by China's 'betrayal' of 'world revolution', the Ruba'i faction improved relations with the Soviet Union. Yet even as they welcomed Soviet assistance, they did not want to become completely dependent upon it and continued to be critical of the Soviets' opportunist policy. Suspicions of alleged Soviet influence in the army caused Ruba'i's radicals to strengthen the People's Militia on the Chinese model and with Chinese aid. (Chinese arms and a Chinese military delegation had already reached Aden at the beginning of 1971.)[9] The PDRY security services, known for their efficiency, power and ruthlessness, were organized with East German financial support and by East German experts.

Soviet assistance was far more diversified and sophisticated than Chinese and included large quantities of relatively modern arms either given or sold at a great discount on long-term credit.[10] South Yemeni officers, technicians and pilots were trained in the USSR, and Soviet experts built military installations in the PDRY and trained its military forces.[11]

Pressure was exerted by the Soviets to be given rights for bases and the use of facilities. Officially, there were no Soviet military bases in the PDRY and, unlike Egypt before July 1972, military installations used by the Soviets were under South Yemeni control. No known agreement concerning the grant of bases to the Soviets was signed. But as Soviet experts were engaged in building ports and military bases, or in maintaining former British ones for the South Yemeni military forces, at least in theory, Soviet ships or planes could always make use of them, because they were run by their own experts and technicians and were supplied with stocks of suitable parts. Thus, unofficially, the Soviets had bases at their disposal, plus most of the services that such bases could provide, without the political disadvantages of an official acknowledgement.[12]

As a corollary to the USSR's increasing interest in the Persian Gulf and its naval presence in the northwest part of the Indian Ocean came a growing interest in the port of Aden. Aden was the most suitable location in the area for a military base, as facilities for the upkeep and repair of ships already existed and it was administered, or at least serviced, by Soviet technicians. On the other hand, the South Yemenis attempted, as much as possible, to keep everything under their own control, restricting the Soviet role to technical aid and advice. With the consequent uncertainty that South Yemeni ports, and Aden in particular, could be used in time of need, the Soviets continued their efforts to diversify their dependence in this area and searched for similar service rights in other places, particularly Somalia.[13]

By 1971, Soviet economic assistance to South Yemen was said to exceed 25 million roubles ($27.5 million) annually, 32 per cent of which was a grant, the rest a long-term loan.[14] This marked increase in aid over the Republic's first years was undoubtedly a Soviet reaction to pressures exerted on the PDRY after 1970, by Saudi Arabia in particular. But the amount was still small considering the PDRY's strategic importance and in comparison to that given to Egypt and Syria by the USSR. Moreover, it was evident that the PDRY leaders themselves closed all options and made themselves completely dependent on the USSR. The Chinese might give them 'Little Red Books' and revolutionary slogans, but no more. The resultant extremism and isolation prevented them from receiving Arab or Western aid.

Saudi Arabia tried to establish a cordon sanitaire around the PDRY and supported local forces conspiring to overthrow its regime. In the last months of 1971, South Yemen's armed forces overwhelmed guerrilla strongholds along its northern border, to prevent or deter the YAR from joining the Saudi camp. For its part, the PDRY stepped up subversive and terrorist activities, for which 'Abdul Fattah Isma'il was largely responsible, against the YAR. By adopting this policy the PDRY in fact played into Saudi hands enabling Saudi Arabia to consolidate its neighbours. Guerrilla warfare along the PDRY borders was expanded in the second half of 1972 and its isolation accentuated.

In November 1972, under Libyan pressure, the presidents of the YAR and the PDRY signed an agreement unifying their countries. Unrealistic because the agreement disregarded the basic factors which had given rise to the crisis, it did temporarily defuse tension between the two Yemens. President Ruba'i's supporters were in fact hostile to the plan. Partly motivated by a factional struggle in the NLF, they were also apprehensive that the more populous and less doctrinaire (if not 'reactionary') YAR would submerge the PDRY, annul its socio-economic achievements and reverse its revolutionary ideology. Ironically, it was Ruba'i's policy rather than Isma'il's which coincided with the Soviet Union's interests. The USSR feared that Isma'il's aggressiveness towards the YAR would only serve the interests of the USSR's enemies by creating a dangerous confrontation in this sensitive region. Generally opposed to traditional 'middle-class' pan-Arabism, the Soviet Union was unsympathetic in principle to the unification of Yemen, which might lead to the erosion of Soviet influence and the loss of facilities in the PDRY.

President Ruba'i concurred in the Soviet view that Isma'il's position on the matter of unity with North Yemen was misguided. After internal NLF struggles Ruba'i gained the upper hand over Isma'il – just when Soviet attention was turning south – from the Eastern Mediterranean, and from Egypt in particular, giving relations with the PDRY much greater importance. During President Ruba'i's visit to the USSR on November 15–21, 1972, his conversations with Soviet leaders dealt with the following subjects, according to TASS (November 21, 1972):

(a) 'further expansion and deepening of Soviet–Yemeni state relations';

(b) inter-party NLF–CPSU relations;

(c) current international problems, with particular attention to the situation in the South of Arabia.

The last was worded carefully so that each side could interpret it as it wished. On the one hand, the Soviets wanted to give NLF leaders the impression that they sided with them, yet on the other they sought to avoid offending conservative Arabian Peninsula regimes. They wanted to make PFLOAG (already receiving its aid primarily from the Soviets) believe it was sounder policy to rely on the USSR than on the CPR, and at the same time to reassure Persian Gulf rulers that the Soviets were not engaged in subversion and did not support those who were.

Because of the 1973 oil crisis the Soviets attached even more importance to relations with the PDRY, increasing its aid to enable the PDRY to withstand external Western and local pressures. United States' efforts to regain lost positions and to strengthen conservative regimes, the increased pressures on the PFLOAG, the tremendous growth in Iranian and Saudi Arabian power and gigantic arms deals with Western powers, all stimulated Soviet efforts to consolidate their position, increase arms supplies and attempt greater cooperation between and among their allies, particularly the PDRY and Iraq. This was the background of the visit to the USSR in March 1973 by PDRY Prime Minister and Defence Minister 'Ali Nassir Muhammad. He also visited Hungary, Czechoslovakia and Poland, where he was promised $32 million in loans and aid worth $5 million.[15]

In September 1973, it was reported that the PDRY had applied for membership to the Soviet bloc's Council for Mutual Economic Assistance (CMEA).[16] Neither the USSR nor other COMECON members appeared very enthusiastic about this report, as it probably reminded them of another radical overseas country, Cuba, into whose economy they had had to pour endless amounts of resources badly needed for themselves.

During the Yom Kippur War, the PDRY helped close the Bab al-Mandab Straits to Israeli navigation. Arab use of oil as a weapon during and after that war and the consequences thereof made relations with the PDRY and its routes to the oil resources very important. While the USSR played a relatively passive role in the oil crisis and its propaganda had little effect on developments, the Soviets could and indeed did claim that their mere presence in the area made the Western powers think twice; it prevented them from forcing the oil-producing countries into accepting Western 'diktats', because the producers knew that they could always have Soviet aid and protection if needed. However, it soon became clear to the Soviets that this assumption did not reflect the actual situation since Saudi Arabia, the UAE and Kuwait did not rely on the USSR by any means and nor did Egypt which had been so heavily supported by them in the October 1973 war. Nevertheless, the Soviet position in the PDRY remained strong because its leaders badly needed the USSR's aid to withstand the heavy pressure from their neighbours (encouraged by America and the growing Iranian forces active in Dhufar).[17]

The importance of the PDRY to Arab strategy against Israel was revealed to Arab states during the October 1973 war. The closure of the Bab al-Mandab Straits to Israeli shipping motivated efforts to integrate the PDRY more strongly into joint Arab activities against Israel. But, while 'moderate' Arab governments became convinced that the PDRY danger to their regimes was limited, the USSR's presence there attracted not only Western attention and the desire for a balancing presence but also threatened to impede joint Arab activities. Anxiety increased particularly with the appearance of reports in 1974 about the stationing of Soviet forces on the island of Perim at the entrance to the Bab al-Mandab Straits, in addition to the increasing Soviet military presence in Somalia.

In the PDRY too the trend to improve relations with the Arab countries and receive economic aid from the oil producers became increasingly stronger. Ironically, it was advocated by Ruba'i 'Ali who was ready to lend his support even at the expense of spreading revolution, while 'Abdul Fattah Isma'il continued to stand for an aggressive revolutionary policy in relation to North Yemen, the Dhufar rebellion, the Gulf regimes and to a certain extent, towards other 'moderate' Arab states. It was probably an extension of his traditional pro-Soviet policy, as well as his particular position as a North Yemeni in South Yemen. His more extreme views strengthened his crumbling position temporarily. But the enormous riches of the oil-producing states, the expected income from the re-opening of the Suez Canal and the change in Soviet policy seemed to balance the scales in favour of Ruba'i 'Ali's faction and policy, resulting in greater cooperation with other Arab countries during 1975 and 1976.[18] It also brought Kuwaiti and Egyptian aid, a diminution of tension with the new 'revolutionary' regime of North Yemen, and led to the establishment of diplomatic relations with Saudi Arabia.

Saudi Arabia too developed a new policy towards the PDRY ('re-

Arabization'), hoping that moderation would effect the removal of the Soviets and the rise of a less extremist PDRY leadership. However, despite the PDRY's readiness to receive aid from anyone ready to provide it, and to pursue both Marxist and Arab nationalist policies, it did not appear likely that even Ruba'i 'Ali would leave the path of the socialist revolution and turn to 'bourgeois' Arab nationalism. South Yemeni cooperation with other Arab countries could therefore continue mainly for long as pan-Arab activity was directed against Israel or the West – and was in the PDRY's interest. Provision of Arab financial aid to the PDRY (according to press reports, promised at the Rabat Arab summit conference in October 1974) was hoped to lead to the weakening of the Soviet position.

The Arab position described above was accompanied by an Egyptian wish to have complete control over the Suez Canal after its re-opening. It was manifested by Egypt's interest in leasing the island of Perim, which controls the Bab al-Mandab Straits to prevent a Soviet presence there. Should hostilities between the Arab countries and Israel break out anew, the Egyptians have taken into account the possibility that their interests would not necessarily be identical with the USSR's. Soviet presence in the Straits could mean a degree of Soviet control over the entrance to the Red Sea and the Suez Canal and thus give them the capacity to exert pressure on Egypt. Be that as it may, the Egyptians have succeeded in convincing Saudi Arabia of the importance of strengthening solidarity with the PDRY, binding it more strongly to other Arab countries than to the USSR by providing financial, political and, if necessary, military aid. The Saudis also hoped that improved relations with the PDRY would lead to a decrease of the pressure on Oman and indirectly to an Iranian withdrawal from that country. In order to be effective such aid had to be greater than that given by the USSR (which increased during 1975–6). It led invariably to closer relations between the PDRY, Saudi Arabia, and other Gulf principalities and the exchange of top-level visits. The competition for influence over the PDRY certainly increased its bargaining power,[19] and diminished its dependence on the USSR. In the long run, it may have a moderating effect on the regime, if it continues to hold power, but at the present time there is no sign that it has affected its internal policy and ideology as its leadership still maintains strong ties with the Soviets, supports Marxist rebels in Eritrea[20] and to some extent supports the Oman rebellion.

The Soviets believe that modernization and education will usher in 'progressive' changes in the Persian Gulf oil-producing regimes, a process they try to accelerate by supporting subversive movements. But as the Soviets have a strong interest in building and maintaining good relations with any regimes in power, it was convenient to have someone else engage in subversion with only indirect Soviet support, for which the USSR could bear no responsibility. The PDRY performed this function by using some of its Soviet aid to subvert neighbouring countries.

Thus far, the PDRY regime has succeeded in maintaining its political and ideological independence. The USSR hopes that by improving relations and infiltrating the NLF regime a swing will result to the Soviet view and lead to an acceptance of CPSU leadership, a development to be bolstered by military dependence and Soviet penetration of the ruling party, trade unions, professional organizations and management of development projects.

After the isolation their revolutionary fervour created, the PDRY was left with little support from any source but the USSR, a situation they later thoroughly encouraged. Recently, recognition of their potential dilemma and the unwillingness of the Soviets to grant them massive economic aid has prompted the PDRY to develop more flexibility by improving relations with other Arab states. Although the economic aid of Saudi Arabia and its allies and the development of closer diplomatic relations with them did not cause a noticeable change in the PDRY's relations with the USSR, the new situation and the resources of the Arab oil producers should serve as writing on the wall for the credibility of the Soviet allies in the region and the erosion of Soviet influence in the Middle East in general.

CHAPTER IX

Power Rivalry in the Indian Ocean

Two basic and interrelated factors are turning the Indian Ocean into a major zone of power rivalry for the coming decade. The first is Persian Gulf oil and the second is the strategic advantage (or disadvantage) emanating from a presence, power balance, or military–tactical hegemony in the region.

Lying between Australia, Asia and Africa, the Indian Ocean is clearly of immense importance to the superpowers, Europe and Japan, as well as the countries on its immediate periphery. After a Soviet flotilla entered in 1968, there has been a gradual Red Sea/ Indian Ocean build-up of a strategic infrastructure directly connected to Soviet aspirations in the Persian Gulf.

Several Western analysts strongly support the thesis that the Soviet naval presence in the northwest Indian Ocean was part of a defensive strategy, as the area (especially the Arabian Sea) is ideally suited to deploying US nuclear submarines (armed since 1967 with the Polaris A-3 – range, 2,500 nautical miles – and, in recent years with the even longer range, multi-warhead Poseidon missiles) which could threaten the Soviet Union's 'soft underbelly'. In this view, Soviet actions are seen as largely a result of the provocative character of Western (mainly US) activity in the region.[1] Naturally, such opinions have been welcomed by the Soviet mass media in its efforts to counter the newly-developing Western naval strategy in the Indian Ocean.

In the 1950s and early 1960s, scholars, journalists and politicians tended to see a Machiavellian scheme behind every tactical move of the Soviet Union. In recent years the general tendency is opposite: as the SALT talks continue and with the importance attributed to the détente policy, there is a tendency to minimize Soviet actions and occasionally overlook altogether Soviet global strategy and ideology; to forget that Soviet activity is utterly pragmatic when it comes to

I

tactics and even strategy and may change according to circumstances. But its fundamental motivation and ideology have remained as dogmatic as ever.

Geoffrey Jukes, in his very interesting article 'The Indian Ocean in Soviet Naval Policy'[2] minimizes, inter alia, the ability and intention of the Soviet flotilla in the Indian Ocean to threaten Western interests in the region. He dismisses the correlation between its presence and Persian Gulf oil. This thesis was challenged by Mordechai Abir in 'Red Sea Politics',[3] in which Abir examined the gradual Soviet build-up in the area and its connection with Soviet aims in the Persian Gulf.

Using Egypt as a proxy, the USSR as early as the late 1950s, had begun its drive to reach the open waters of the Indian Ocean and the Persian Gulf, and to build its strategic infrastructure in the Red Sea. It was more than coincidence that the Soviet Navy reached the Gulf of Aden in 1968, just after the British announced their 'east of Suez' policy and their intention of withdrawing from the Persian Gulf. The offensive character of this infrastructure and of the flotilla maintained by the Soviets in the Indian Ocean is rarely questioned today. The Soviets exploited their navy to expand and strengthen their influence and position in the region ('showing the flag') and to obtain further facilities and bases in the countries surrounding the Indian Ocean even before the re-opening of the Suez Canal, mainly in Somalia and to some extent in the PDRY.[4] Substantially strengthened, the Soviet Indian Ocean fleet has led, among other things, to the acquisition of additional facilities in island-states such as Seychelles, Mauritius, Reunion and Comoro. It also helped strengthen political parties in the countries of the Indian Ocean which readily cooperate with the Soviet Union. Despite the pragmatic tactics of the USSR and the low profile which it is now desperately trying to project concerning its presence in the Indian Ocean, Soviet strategy is clearly aimed at achieving at least parity with the West, and therefore some of their first carriers must be destined to strengthen their navy in the Indian Ocean.[5] This policy is already having a far-reaching impact on the local and even the international strategic balance, not to mention the fuel supply complex.

Even if we overlook the effect on local politics of 'showing the flag', several factors make the Indian Ocean essential for Russian defence and extremely attractive to Soviet strategic planning. The first is obviously the Persian Gulf, which contains about half of the world's proven oil reserves and which is the West's most important source of fuel. Although recent Soviet naval 'war games' in mid-1975 (Okean) indicated intentions of attacking Western oil routes in the Indian Ocean and South Atlantic,[6] it is unlikely that the Soviets would try to interfere directly with the flow of oil to the West as such an act would be completely incompatible with Soviet détente policy and is far beyond their occasional brinkmanship policy. However, such caution would not prevent the USSR from doing as much as possible to erode the position of Western oil companies and Western interests in the Gulf region.

It is only logical to assume that the Soviet naval presence in the Indian Ocean has had a not inconsiderable influence on OPEC's policy since 1970, especially in relation to oil prices and the use of the 'oil weapon' by the Arab oil producers in October 1973. It is inconceivable that the oil-producing countries would have taken such extreme steps without considering possible Western reaction, and they knew that such a reaction would be mitigated by the presence of the Soviet navy not far from the Persian Gulf. Although it is unlikely that the Soviet Union would have done more than protest verbally against 'action' in the Gulf in the event of a real threat to the Western energy supply and economy, the Soviet presence in the Indian Ocean did force the West to weigh carefully the steps it was prepared to take.

In the last decade, the oceans have become a pillar of nuclear strategy and the Indian Ocean is part of the Soviet defensive and offensive complexes. Surrounded by three continents, it is extremely important, especially in the context of a US second strike capability against the USSR (although now with the advent of Trident nuclear submarines and the new MIRV missiles, not more important than several other stretches of the high sea, as some analysts claim).

One cannot overlook the fact that many nations, with a substantial part of the Third World's population, border on the Indian Ocean and relations with them are important to the Soviet Union. This fact is also related to the Sino-Soviet conflict. The USSR has a profound fear of China and therefore the Soviet presence in the Indian Ocean is at least partly connected with strategic plans concerning mainland China.[7] For their part, the Chinese have a traumatic fear of being engulfed and crushed by a Soviet 'pincer' movement, and assume Soviet activities in the Indian Ocean are part of such a strategy. They fear that the re-opened Suez Canal will make them even more vulnerable. It is not surprising, therefore, that the Chinese bitterly attack Soviet 'naval imperialism' in the Indian Ocean and that they strongly, although not publicly, opposed the re-opening of the Canal.

The re-opening of the Suez Canal no doubt affords the Soviet Union important strategic and economic advantages. It is not a mere cliché that the shortest route from the USSR to the USSR is via the Suez Canal. Moreover, it would provide the USSR with the shortest route between the Black Sea and the Indian Ocean (2,200 miles from the USSR's Black Sea ports to Aden, compared to 12,000 miles around the Cape and about 9,000 miles from Vladivostok). Thus, the Soviet Union will be able to save a substantial number of ship-days and deploy all its fleets more efficiently and economically than in the past. Furthermore, the ability to rotate naval units between different fleets is extremely important for Soviet naval strategy (as is constantly demonstrated in the Mediterranean and the Atlantic). Although still dependent on air cover from facilities and bases acquired from the countries of the Indian Ocean (the new Soviet carriers of the Kiev class are just over 40,000 tons DW and will be able to sail through the Canal). Furthermore, it is well known that time and cost factors are completely irrelevant to Soviet planners when an objective is given a sufficiently high priority. In fact, even before the Yom Kippur War, the Soviet Indian Ocean fleet grew dramatically in absolute number of vessels and ship-days and comprised missile-carrying cruisers, destroyers, nuclear and conventional submarines, and smaller craft and auxiliaries.[8]

Until 1970 it appeared as though the United States was ignoring developments in the Indian Ocean and the Red Sea. It firmly believed that the 'policing' of the Gulf should be left to its local allies – Iran and Saudi Arabia – and that the Soviet Union would not dare penetrate this sensitive area. The United States ignored the Soviet fleet in the Gulf of Aden and the growing Soviet strategic infrastructure, and was even instrumental in the agreement between Egypt and Israel which facilitated the re-opening of the Canal in 1975, on the assumption that while the impact on the strategic balance in the Indian Ocean would be minimal, it was important to the economy of Europe and the Persian Gulf region, and to the solution of the Arab–Israeli conflict. Since 1971, however, the United States has initiated steps to contain Soviet power and halt the spread of Soviet influence in areas the West considers crucial. In addition, the United States began to build up a communications and 'facilities' network stretching from Cockburn Sound in Western Australia to East Africa. Following the signing of the Soviet–Iraqi treaty of April 1972, these steps were accelerated in view of the rapid growth from that time onwards of Soviet naval power, facilities, and base network in the Indian Ocean.

The energy crisis at the beginning of 1973 caused a further escalation in the superpowers' activities in the Indian Ocean. It is possible that the October War may have somewhat accelerated developments in the region, but it was not the cause of the 'energy crisis' or of related developments. The appearance of the American flotilla, detached from the Seventh Fleet, not far from Bab al-Mandab, was no doubt an important departure from past policy. But it was only a question of time before an American naval force would have been sent to the area in view of the American re-evaluation of Soviet intentions in the region, the deterioration of the situation there and Western anxiety caused by the substantial growth of Soviet power and influence in the Indian Ocean.

A new American strategy (mainly naval-oriented) has gradually emerged following a re-evaluation of the changed situation. Clearly the Persian Gulf (in accordance with the US departure from its previous land-oriented strategy) is not important per se, but only in relation to its oil and America's Indian Ocean strategy. The United States realized that it could not fully rely on its local allies in the Persian Gulf to contain the Soviet Union. Willing to enjoy the American protective umbrella, these allies clearly valued their own interests far above those of the West.[9] The ramifications of the new situation were clear when the Arabs used the 'oil weapon' during and after the October War. The fact that the Americans did not have a meaningful presence in the Indian Ocean greatly narrowed the range of options which were open to them. Further, when the American flotilla, including an aircraft carrier, reached the north-western part of the Ocean, it met many difficulties, as it was unable to use facilities or a base in the area and its home base, Subic Bay (Philippines) was 7,000 miles away. In contrast to the Soviet navy the mainstay of the US navy is aircraft carriers, very few of which can use the Canal because they are too large. Therefore the American flotilla in the Indian Ocean must continue to sail from the Pacific (Seventh Fleet).

In order to maintain their presence in a crucially important area, to counter the Soviet presence and protect Western oil supplies, the

United States decided to construct a naval and air base in the Indian Ocean. The choice fell upon Diego Garcia, ideally situated in the middle of the Indian Ocean opposite the Gulf, a British base where the Americans had already established an important communications centre. Other British bases used occasionally by the US are Masiva, Gan and the Mahé islands. In fact, after the plan was approved by the American Congress (1975), Diego Garcia may become part of a complex of air and naval bases between Africa and Australia, with the cooperation of the British, French and Iranians. Such a chain of bases, in addition to the fact that the approaches to the Indian Ocean from the east and northwest are controlled by straits, could nullify a good part of the advantage gained by the Soviets through the re-opening of the Canal and their consequent ability to rotate and reinforce their fleets. It will also be extremely important for US second strike capability.

The new American militancy in the Indian Ocean, their greater involvement in the Gulf and Arabia and their efforts to erode Soviet influence in the Middle East as a whole as well as in the Indian sub-continent, brought an immediate reaction from the Soviet Union. In addition to the outcry in the Soviet mass media over American escalation of the situation, the Soviets encouraged their allies in and around the Indian Ocean to condemn US 'neo-imperialism'; isolationist and anti-militaristic circles in the United States and Europe are also being used to protest against the 'adventurist plans' of the US military establishment in the Indian Ocean.[10] While 'crying wolf', the USSR has nevertheless been strengthening its position in Somalia, East Africa, the PDRY, and until recently in Iraq (it failed to gain new concessions from India) and is methodically expanding its facilities in island-states in the Indian Ocean. At the same time it has determined to lower its profile in the Ocean and generally stop subversive activities against conservative oil regimes, which in any case contribute indirectly towards Soviet power.

The re-opening of the Suez Canal did not bring an immediate and dramatic change in the strategic balance in the Indian Ocean. In the age of nuclear deterrents and the balance of fear, capability and power are not measured by the resources available in the area, but rather by the sum total of the resources available to a power and the options open before it. On the other hand, the age of conventional weapons and forces is far from over, as both superpowers are discovering. Within the margins open to superpowers, in a limited conflict conventional forces can prove extremely useful and efficient – a lesson both superpowers are learning in the northwestern part of the Indian Ocean. 'Navies, while indispensable (for) armed combat, are also constantly being utilized as an instrument of state policy in peacetime', writes Admiral Gorshkov.[11]

The coming years will probably be crucial for the West in relation to its economy and energy supply, and the Gulf and the Indian Ocean's importance will grow accordingly. It is expected that even if the détente policy is continued, each superpower will try, nevertheless, to strengthen its position in the region and to undermine the other's within the permissible limits of conflict and rivalry.

Within the context of the new global naval strategy pursued by the Soviets[12] it has become more important for the USSR to control the sea lanes to and from the Gulf than to control the Gulf itself. Thus, controlling the passage of oil is as important as controlling the source of oil. The significance of this is substantial because at least until the end of the 1970s the Soviets have the advantage of internal lines of communication, whereas the West must become increasingly dependent on transporting fuel by sea. Now that Mozambique (and Angola) are independent, the Soviets are likely to endeavour to expand their presence to the strategic Mozambique Channel. Moreover, because the likelihood is relatively remote of their gaining control over the eastern approaches to the Indian Ocean, Soviet attempts to encourage changes in the southern part of Africa and establish some influence in this strategic region ought not to be overlooked.

CHAPTER X

Trends and Considerations

A. SOVIET DECISION-MAKING AND AIMS

The foreign relations of any country and particularly the USSR strongly reflect internal politics and power rivalries. For the Soviet leaders it is imperative that the Soviet Union prevail in the international arena, but what really matters most to them is their position within the power structure of their country. It is difficult, therefore, to separate leading Soviet personalities' views on any particular foreign issue from internal Soviet factors.

It is assumed that generalizations concerning the attitudes and policies of Western regimes representing open, democratic, pluralistic societies do not reflect an entire spectrum of opinion within each country or even within the government. Despite the difference in regime, the same is true of the USSR. To say 'the USSR wants' or 'the Soviets think' is very much a generalization, as various factions and individual members of the Soviet leadership may together hold a spectrum of opinions on the same matter. The decision-making apparatus of the Soviet Union is cautious and slow-moving but is not as monolithic as it appears. Obviously, there are policy decisions and ideological constraints which must be followed: official CPSU, politbureau or Central Committee decisions, resolutions or statements, or even *Pravda* editorials which seem to represent the official position. But even these are often variously interpreted by those who must implement them and are adapted to circumstances, conditions and situations. Those at the top who must decide are very often only superficially aware of the actual situation and are completely dependent on facts and analysis presented to them by subordinates. Mismanagement and disorder are not rare, one official or government agency may not know what the other does or may even follow different lines of action. In relation to the Middle East it may happen, therefore, that one Soviet representative calls for moderation, while another supports an extreme position. This is not only the result of a division of functions, but more often represents different positions and interests of internal Soviet power groups of which little is known outside the USSR.

Taking into consideration the above-mentioned qualifications, there is still some doubt as to what the Soviets actually want to achieve in the Middle East, how they perceive developments, their future presence and relations with the local regimes, as well as with foreign powers involved in the area. It is well to distinguish between tactical moves such as détente with the United States, and long-range strategy and ideology. Generally, the Soviets are not much influenced by the time element and, seeing issues in an historical perspective, are ready to bide their time and to wait for 'inevitable' trends or processes. It is also necessary to distinguish between: (a) doctrinal–ideological considerations of the Soviet Union as the leading communist power, its missionary aims and ambitions to spread the 'faith' whenever and wherever possible, and (b) the military–political–economic interests of the USSR as a state and superpower, although in some instances the two may coincide.

In the first role, the USSR sees itself as head of the world's revolutionary forces, protecting and supporting 'just', 'anti-imperialist' struggles. At times this role may conflict with its national interests. Generally, the Soviets extensively employ 'revolutionary' phraseology and its declared aims and policies are apparently closer to a doctrinal–ideological posture. In reality, since Stalin's death in 1953, policy is no longer the outcome of the purely doctrinal approach, but rather the immediate interests of Russia. Therefore it is empiric and cautious. Or that is to say, Soviet policy should be seen not only in the light of what they say, but by what they do.

In examining Soviet policy it is also necessary to distinguish between strategy and tactics. The first is dogmatic and linked to the aims of communism, the second, extremely pragmatic. The aims may be long-term, intermediate or short-term. Long-range aims are strategic, far-reaching and relate to a messianic future, but are not binding on current conduct or policy. Intermediate and short-term goals are more tactical, are not always ends in themselves but a method of achieving future aims, and therefore more flexible and realistic. Today's intermediate aims may seem only marginally feasible, whereas short-term aims are intended to be realizable.

As pragmatists, the Soviets are well aware of the constraints in relation to the Persian Gulf and its environs resulting from détente, Western interests in the area and their limited technological–economic ability to compete with the West. This accurate appraisal of the situation makes it easier for the Soviets to bridge the gap between ideals and what is possible to attain without abandoning their long-term view.

The Soviets see their position in the Middle East in a far more optimistic light than do others. They believe that many factors exist in the region that can be exploited for developing their policy and aims: (a) political asymmetries; (b) internal tensions; (c) tension between oil producers and Arab nationalism and Western oil consumers; (d) the weakness and instability of regional regimes; (e) the division of the Arab world into 'haves' and 'have-nots'; (f) the need to modernize archaic societies quickly; (g) the Third World's disappointment with the democratic system; (h) the existence (albeit limited) of a class-conscious proletariat and a large community of under-privileged immigrants, often lacking even basic civil rights.

Soviet aims concerning the Middle East and the Gulf may be classified as follows:

Long-term: Establishment of a universal communist regime; the time element is irrelevant. In the Middle East this would entail:

1. Turning the area into the southern tier of a socialist commonwealth under the USSR.

2. Control over Persian Gulf oil and integration of its production into COMECON planning.

3. Establishing land links from the USSR to the Indian Ocean, to diminish Soviet dependence on passage through the Turkish Straits, the Suez Canal and around Africa.

Intermediate aims: (Attainable with time, social and political changes):

1. A 'Finlandization' of the area. The countries of the area would retain their independence, 'determine' their regimes and their internal affairs, but would have to 'coordinate' their foreign relations with the USSR. A *pax Sovietica*, preventing local conflicts, would be maintained with the assistance of those in whose favour the Soviets resolve the area's disputes.

2. Establishment of local, revolutionary–progressive, anti-Western and pro-Soviet regimes, preferably ideologically close to the Soviet

Union. Such regimes would nationalize Western economic interests (particularly oil), increase trade with the Soviet Union, purchase Soviet arms and be integrated in the Soviet defence system.

3. A limited Soviet military presence in the area or near it, to prevent crises, coups or other developments detrimental to the USSR's interests.

Short-term aims:

1. To diminish, erode or completely remove the Western presence and influence, political, military and economic. To exploit and expand, towards that end, differences between the local regimes and the West, mainly America.

2. To undermine traditional regimes and assist the emergence of 'progressive' pro-Soviet ones.

3. To prevent Chinese penetration into the area.

4. To build a military infrastructure in the region, expanding where and whenever possible the Soviet military presence, and demonstrate Soviet power by showing the flag.

5. To erode Western military power and, or second-strike capability.

6. To expand Soviet commercial links (including air connections, overflight and refuelling rights and other facilities), for their own sake as well as for political and military aims.

7. To use the Middle East in the wider sense as a springboard for achievements elsewhere.

B. CONCLUSION: THE USSR AND THE MIDDLE EAST

When the Soviets first entered the Arab world, they were confident, boasting that they would succeed where others had failed: not only did they have a better understanding of the area, its problems and needs, but they had much more to offer. Yet, confronted by the problems previously faced by the West, they often came up with similar answers. They preferred quick industrialization and 'transition to socialism' to solve the area's problems, but soon realized that such solutions would require many years. The Russians gradually became aware of the significant psychological, cultural and social differences between themselves, as Europeans, and oriental peoples, and that they had failed to appreciate the impact of factors such as nationalism, religion, tribal and family allegiances, illiteracy and economic backwardness. They discovered that the Arabs' approach to problems could be very different from their own, as was their way of thinking, and that although they often used the same terms, each interpreted them differently.

The Soviets believed in a gradual transition from one stage in social development to another. The pace of transition, they claimed, chiefly depended on local conditions and socio-economic developments. Some countries might (with Soviet aid) skip over certain stages and evolve directly from feudalism to socialism. This, the Soviets pointed out, had occurred in the Soviet central Asian republics (predominantly Muslim) and could be achieved elsewhere, perhaps in the PDRY and Somalia.

According to Soviet analyses, Saudi Arabia, Qatar and the UAE have 'patriarchal–feudal' regimes. Yemen has advanced one stage higher and is just entering the stage of capitalism. Kuwait and Bahrayn are rated higher in the capitalist stage, as they have a proletariat and an emerging class conflict. In Iran the 'national bourgeoisie' is considered to have succeeded in overcoming the feudals and (to some extent) the *'compradore bourgeoisie'*, who represent foreign interests, and has achieved some measure of independence. Iraq has developed the state sector of the economy and appears to be turning from capitalism to a 'non-capitalist' development. The PDRY is advancing directly from feudalism to socialism, jumping over the capitalist stage. All this appears highly schematic and does not necessarily conform to reality. It reflects nevertheless Soviet views and influences their attitude to the Persian Gulf.

Soviet policy in the Middle East, focused initially on communist parties and related 'frontal organizations', was found to be leading nowhere. The relatively few communists in those countries exerted no influence and their support was worthless. The Soviets therefore turned to other 'revolutionaries' and anti-Western elements: Ba'athists in Iraq and Syria, Nasser in Egypt, NLF leaders in the PDRY. These were now termed 'progressives' or 'revolutionary democrats' and were given political, military and economic aid. Once in power, they were expected to act as communists or expected to so act with time. In most cases, however, this approach proved disappointing as the Soviets discovered that the leaders of most Arab countries set a high price on their cooperation, wasted Soviet aid, and lacked a sense of gratitude. Eventually, the Soviet leadership decided to adapt themselves to reality and turned to traditional and conventional inter-state relations. They gave up the previous policy of attempting to fill any vacuum, became more selective and their efforts were focused on only those areas and countries of particular interest to themselves and which held a promise of a quick return.

The aftermath of the 'oil crisis' of 1973, especially its ruinous impact on Western economy, revived Soviet hopes. Without lifting a finger, they gained a tremendous strategic victory and some economic advantage, while the West suffered an enormous strategic and economic blow. The Soviets watched this process gleefully, claiming it part of the decline of Western capitalism – which they have always predicted. But in order to ensure the continuity of the process, they systematically strove to strengthen their presence and influence in the Gulf environs, although exercising prudence even after the re-opening of the Suez Canal in 1975 and maintaining a relatively low profile of their naval power in the Indian Ocean (which they can reinforce in a relatively brief period).

While Soviet gains through the change in the oil market are mainly strategic, their economic gains are not to be dismissed. The rise in oil prices and greater Soviet involvement in oil marketing coincided with the shift of the centre of gravity of the Soviet oil industry eastwards to Siberia where production and transportation to the centres of consumption are more costly. These costs, plus the rise in price of Western products the USSR required to purchase, were compensated by the Soviets' increased revenue as a net oil exporter (one estimate is that USSR's oil sales reached $5 billion in 1974/75). Yet the other COMECON countries must now pay much more for their oil importation and by the 1980s the USSR itself may become a net oil importer, also dependent on expensive oil from the Gulf. Moreover, Soviet hopes that the United States would participate extensively in the development of Siberian oil and gas resources did not materialize. Though it wishes to diversify its sources of supply and diminish its dependence on one source, the United States fears that the Russians, like the Arabs, may use oil as a political–strategic weapon. Obviously, it prefers to be dependent for its oil on the weak Arab countries rather than on its powerful rival, the USSR.

Although the major oil-producing countries represented in OPEC are generally considered pro-Western, there is some correlation between their policy and interests, especially in regards to oil, and those of the Soviets. Most producers are aware that they have relatively limited time at their disposal to get as much as possible of the industrialized countries' wealth and to diversify their own economies. Even here the interests of the big conservative producers are at odds with those of the West, but in contrast to the 'progressive' and less important producers, they desire to cooperate with the West because they need Western help to defend themselves against external and internal threats and Western technology for their economic development. With a population of less than five million and lacking the infrastructure to absorb its vast oil revenues, Saudi Arabia's oil policy is based on long-range considerations and seems both 'realistic' and amicable to the West. Its regime comprehends that it would be foolhardy to push the lethargic Western leadership into a corner – not to mention the danger that the complete erosion of Western power would create to the oil countries' conservative regimes. It supports, therefore, an oil policy which the West can tolerate, at the same time preserving the producers' interests, unity and power.

There is little doubt that Saudi Arabia's prudent oil policy and apparent willingness to cooperate with the United States paid dividends. Talk about Western intervention in the Gulf subsided in 1975, while no serious Western energy policy has been developed beyond the establishment (in 1975) of the relatively powerless 'International Energy Agency' (IEA), which agreed about minimal oil prices (to prevent the producers from sabotaging the development of alternative sources of energy) and the pooling of oil resources in periods of emergency. Otherwise, the Western powers continue to compete among themselves for the oil producers' petrodollars. The United States, moreover, reduced its efforts to develop substitutes for imported fuel and is becoming increasingly dependent on Gulf oil. This not only renders it more vulnerable to Arab pressures, but also to Soviet leverage resulting from its capacity to threaten the oil routes from the Gulf to Europe and America.

American leaders are confident that the regimes of the conservative oil producers realize that it is in their interests to maintain friendly relations with the West and to supply its oil requirements at acceptable prices. In addition to its undertakings in the field of defence in Iran, the US's involvement in Arabia is increasing and it is now supplying the conservative Arab governments, especially Saudi Arabia, with substantial technical aid and vast quantities of sophisticated weapon systems. (According to a projection of the US Office of Defence, 150,000 Americans will be employed in the Gulf by 1980.)

Events in southeast Asia and Angola eroded American credibility in the world. Although desirous of reducing their dependence on American protection, the conservative Gulf regimes realize that for the present they still need American weapons and protective umbrella – and that the West's dependence on their oil is still the best guarantee against foreign intervention. In this context, they welcome the US's mediation in the Arab–Israeli conflict and its new 'even-handed' policy, aware that a new outbreak of war might force them to use the 'oil weapon' again, perhaps with grave consequences.

For its part, it seems imperative to the United States to prevent a fusion of interests and action between the Soviets and the producers of the Gulf. America has been exploiting the leverage gained after the Yom Kippur War not only to block the Soviets' advance, but to erode previous Soviet gains. The seeming success of this policy has strengthened America's belief in the viability, power and durability of the Teheran–Riyadh–Cairo axis and in the continuing importance of regional 'pro-Western' and 'pro-Soviet' leanings. In addition to the dangers of exaggerating the credibility of this 'axis' and certainties of allegiance, it overlooks the fragility of the foundations of the regimes which have become the pillars of its policy.

Certain parallels exist between the present American policy in the Middle East, especially in regard to an anti-Soviet Teheran–Riyadh–Cairo axis and the doctrines of the 1950s. Dr Kissinger's policy of wooing the Arabs, partly by stressing 'common interests' in political and economic fields and employing 'even-handedness' in the Arab–Israeli conflict, may be seen as a continuation of the policy of late Secretary of State, John Foster Dulles. Though perhaps satisfactory in the 1950s its utility is questionable now that crucial issues are so different.

After 1973, OPEC and especially OAPEC members, discovered their power and wealth were dependent on the ability to maintain their overt unity and cooperation. Ideologies, personal, and historic rivalries lost much of their importance, as did former alliances and allegiances. The classification of Arab and other Middle Eastern countries into 'pro-Western' or 'pro-Soviet', moderate or radical, has become less meaningful. Despite grave differences and conflicting interests, which occasionally surface, every effort is made to maintain the Arab and the oil-producers' solidarity which has proved so profitable. If attitudes concerning the Arab–Israeli conflict are disregarded, the most meaningful classification of Middle Eastern countries today is between the oil 'haves' and the 'have-nots'. Some funds are channelled to the 'have-nots' to keep them in line, to gain their cooperation and limit the ability of the powers to exploit their grudges and frustrations. But with rising confidence, the conservative Arab oil countries have gradually become more daring in their role of arbitrators, manipulating their vast funds and influence in the international arena and even coercing their powerful brethren.

Egypt's policy has become, to some extent, an extrapolation of the Saudi Arabian line, because of its increasing dependence on Saudi aid. It tried, with limited success, to strengthen its influence among the other Persian Gulf countries to ensure the flow of essential financial assistance. Estimated at $5 billion annually for the next ten years, this injection of economic aid is crucial to stop the decline in Egypt's economy. Yet only a relatively small part is forthcoming and President Sadat has already hinted on several occasions that he cannot allow such a situation to continue. Moreover, although it abrogated in 1976 its agreement with the USSR, Egypt is unlikely to receive substantially increased economic aid from the US.

Egypt's dependence on political nonentities, its frustration and growing internal unrest may return it to revolutionary pan-Arabism or social radicalism, thus adopting once again an aggressive foreign policy. If plans supported by Damascus for the creation of a 'Greater Syria' ever come to fruition, the Syrian Ba'ath regime may try eventually to bring oil countries of the Arabian Peninsula under its wing. Such possibilities, still remote, are not seriously enough considered by American policy makers. The United States is willing to sell large quantities of modern weapons to confrontation countries in addition to the substantial sophisticated weaponry already sold to conservative Gulf countries. These weapons and the expansion of the Gulf armies may, however, intensify local conflicts, are already causing meaningful social changes and could spark off processes leading to revolutionary upheavals in the Gulf regimes, even be used for local conflicts and under certain circumstances against the West.

The Soviets have decided at least temporarily to diminish their efforts to gain footholds in the Gulf. This attitude is not only due to Soviet apprehension of the reaction of the Gulf countries, but also, despite their occasional statements to the contrary, because they continue to consider the area outside their sphere of influence and essential to the West. Therefore, so long as the USSR is convinced of Western determination to protect its crucial interests, the USSR is unlikely to intervene in the Gulf, unless its national interest is at stake. The Soviets find it difficult to comprehend that weak, backward countries are able to dictate terms to the West and exploit a factor essential to Western survival. This is interpreted by the Soviets more as an expression of Western weakness than of Arab strength. As time passes, should Western indecision and disunity become more apparent, thereby further eroding credibility, the Soviet attitude regarding the Gulf could harden.

Notwithstanding, the Soviets are reconciled to America's present success in the Middle East, mainly because they believe that it is temporary. In the final analysis, they feel that because of processes already initiated in the countries of the area, time is on their side. Arab aspirations and demands, they believe, are not compatible with Western interests. They argue that unlike the West there are (at least temporarily) no conflicting interests between the USSR and the Arab oil producers. Moreover, should a new Arab–Israeli war break out, the United States, they assume, would again help Israel and the Arabs would again turn to the USSR for aid. But to exacerbate clashes between the oil-producing and oil-consuming countries and take advantage of new developments in the interim it is essential for the USSR to continue to show the flag in the area.

With infinite patience Soviet leaders are willing to await the development of an opportune situation. As far as they are concerned, détente serves to prevent open confrontation with the United States, yet can be exploited wherever possible, especially in the 'grey zones', to expedite their long-range aims. Nonetheless, most Western leaders and scholars persuaded by Soviet pragmatism tend to overlook the ideological motivation and long-range aims of the USSR. The distinction is still between tactics and strategy.

The erosion of Western power remains part of the Soviets' 'grand design' to destroy capitalism and, at least in the coming decade, oil will continue as a major factor in the global struggle for power. Because they consider the conservative Gulf countries anti-communist and friendly to them, America and West Europe invariably overlook the long-term impact of their policy and its contribution to Soviet goals. As far as the USSR is concerned, even if Saudi Arabia, Kuwait

K

or Iran are at present *subjectively* anti-Soviet and anti-communist, *objectively* (to use Soviet terminology) they are only doing what the Russians could not manage or would not dare to do by themselves. What matters is the end result (whether realistic or not): the complete erosion of Western economy and power, leading to the final triumph of communism.

Soviet interest in the Gulf region has been growing in the last few years because of its proximity and strategic location and irrespective of its oil. Even though the USSR has been losing ground in the Middle East, this does not affect their ability to operate in the Indian Ocean either for defensive purposes or, not less important, to threaten the maritime lanes through which the Gulf oil is transported to the West. The importance of this leverage increases in direct relation to the rapid growth of United States' dependence on Gulf oil. Indeed the USSR's presence in the vicinity of the Gulf will become even more important when its need for imported oil materializes.

All in all, their many reverses of the last few years have had a sobering effect upon Soviet policy. Just as the Americans ultimately learned to do, the Soviets are gradually disengaging themselves from previous concepts and, it seems, are turning more and more to the utilization of naval strategy. As more carriers of the 'Kiev' type become operational, a new dimension will be added to the Soviet presence in the Indian Ocean and in the vicinity of the Gulf. In future it is likely that actual physical presence in the Middle East will be far less necessary – which may lead to the development of revolutionary concepts concerning Soviet relations. Such an attitude, if it materializes, could have a devastating effect on Middle Eastern countries, particularly if the two superpowers learn to work together, for their own mutual interests and the benefit of the world. On the other hand, the possible rivalry for Gulf oil could lead to an escalation of the conflict between the powers and further strengthen the leverage of the producers on the world community.

Appendix 1

Treaty of Friendship and Cooperation Between the Union of Soviet Socialist Republics and the Iraqi Republic

The Union of Soviet Socialist Republics and the Iraqi Republic,

firmly convinced that the further development of friendship and all-round cooperation between them accords with the national interests of both states and serves the cause of peace throughout the world and in the area of the Arab countries, the interests of freedom of the peoples, their security and respect for sovereignty,

believing that the strengthening of the solidarity of all forces of peace and progress, including the consolidation of unity of the Arab states, on an anti-imperialist basis is a vital means of the struggle for a lasting peace and international security,

inspired by the ideals of struggle against imperialism, colonialism, Zionism and reaction, for freedom, independence, and social progress of the peoples,

convinced that in the modern world international problems should be settled by means of cooperation and a search for mutually-acceptable solutions,

reaffirming their peaceable foreign policy and allegiance to the aims and principles of the United Nations Charter,

moved by a desire to develop and strengthen the existing relations of friendship, cooperation and mutual trust, and striving to raise these relations to a new, still higher level, have decided to conclude the present Treaty and have agreed on the following:

Article 1.

The High Contracting Parties declare that unbreakable friendship will exist between the two countries and their peoples and all-round cooperation will develop in the political, economic, trade, scientific, technological, cultural and other fields on the basis of respect for state sovereignty, territorial integrity and non-interference in each other's internal affairs.

Article 2.

The Union of Soviet Socialist Republics and the Iraqi Republic declare that they will cooperate closely and in all fields to ensure conditions for preserving and further developing the social and economic gains of their peoples and respect for the sovereignty of each of them over all their natural resources.

Article 3.

The High Contracting Parties, consistently conducting a policy of peaceful coexistence of states with differing social systems, will, in conformity with their peaceable foreign policy, continue to work for universal peace, relaxation of international tension, and general and complete disarmament, embracing both nuclear and conventional types of armaments, under effective international control.

Article 4.

Guided by ideals of freedom and equality of all peoples, the High Contracting Parties condemn imperialism and colonialism in all their forms and manifestations. They will continue to wage a steadfast struggle against imperialism and Zionism, for the complete, final and unconditional liquidation of colonialism and neo-colonialism, racism and apartheid, and to come out for the earliest and total implementation of the UN Declaration on the Granting of Independence to the Colonial Countries and Peoples.

The Parties will cooperate with each other and with other peace-loving states in supporting the just struggle of the peoples for their sovereignty, freedom, independence and social progress.

Article 5.

Attaching great importance to economic, technical and scientific cooperation between them, the High Contracting Parties will continue to expand and deepen such cooperation and exchange of experience in industry, agriculture, irrigation, water conservancy, development of oil and other natural resources, in the sphere of communications and in other sectors of the economy, as well as in the training of national personnel. The Parties will expand trade and shipping between the two states on the basis of the principles of equality, mutual benefit, and most-favoured-nation treatment.

Article 6.

The High Contracting Parties will further promote the development of ties and contacts between them in the fields of science, art, literature, education, health services, the press, radio, cinema, television, tourism, sport and other fields.

The Parties will promote wider cooperation and direct ties between state bodies and public organizations, enterprises, cultural and scientific institutions of both states for the purpose of a deeper mutual acquaintance with the life, work and accomplishments of the peoples of the two countries in various spheres.

Article 7.

Attaching great importance to concerted action in the international arena in the interests of ensuring peace and security, as well as to the development of political cooperation between the Soviet Union and Iraq, the High Contracting Parties will regularly consult each other at different levels on all important international issues affecting the interests of both states, as well as on questions of the further development of bilateral relations.

Article 8.

In the event of the development of situations spelling a danger to peace of either Party or creating a danger to peace or violation of peace, the High Contracting Parties will contact each other without delay in order to agree their positions with a view to removing the threat that has arisen or re-establishing peace.

Article 9.

In the interests of security of both countries, the High Contracting Parties will continue to develop cooperation in the strengthening of their defence capacity.

Article 10.

Each of the High Contracting Parties declares that it will not enter into alliances and will not take part in any groupings of states, in actions or measures directed against the other High Contracting Party.

Each of the High Contracting Parties pledges not to allow its territory to be used for any action to be carried out that would do military harm to the other Party.

Article 11.

The two High Contracting Parties declare that their commitments under existing international treaties are not in contradiction with the provisions of the present Treaty and undertake not to enter into any international agreements incompatible with it.

Article 12.

The present Treaty is concluded for a term of 15 years and will be prolonged automatically for each subsequent five-year period, if neither of the High Contracting Parties declares its desire of terminating its operation, notifying the other High Contracting Party 12 months before the expiring of the term of operation of the Treaty.

Article 13.

Any differences which may arise between the High Contracting Parties in relation to the interpretation of any provision of the present Treaty will be settled bilaterally in a spirit of friendship, mutual respect and understanding.

Article 14.

The present Treaty is subject to ratification and shall come into force on the day of exchange of ratification instruments, which will take place in Moscow in the nearest possible future.

The present Treaty is done in two copies, each in Russian and Arabic, both texts being equally authentic.

K2

Done in the City of Baghdad on April 9, 1972, which corresponds to 25 Safar 1392, Hegira.

For the Union of	For the Iraqi
Soviet Socialist	Republic
Republics	A. H. al-BAKR
A. KOSYGIN	(Pravda, April 10, 1972.)

(*Moscow News*, no. 16, April 15, 1972, Supp.)

Appendix 2

Treaty of Friendship and Cooperation between the Union of Soviet Socialist Republics and the Somali Democratic Republic

The Union of Soviet Socialist Republics and the Somali Democratic Republic,

considering that the further development of friendship and all-round cooperation between them meets the radical national interests of the peoples of both states and serves the cause of strengthening peace throughout the world,

inspired by the ideals of struggle against imperialism and colonialism and the invariable striving to render the utmost support to the peoples fighting for freedom, independence and social progress and to work for the complete abolition of colonialism in all its forms and manifestations,

fully resolved to promote the consolidation of international peace and security in the interests of the peoples of all countries,

convinced that in the world of today international problems should be solved only in a peaceful way,

confirming their fidelity to the aims and principles of the Charter of the United Nations Organization,

motivated by the striving to strengthen and consolidate the relations of friendship and mutually advantageous cooperation which exist between both states and peoples and to create a basis for their further development,

have decided to conclude the present Treaty of Friendship and Cooperation and agreed on the following.

Article 1.

The High Contracting Parties solemnly proclaim that lasting peace and friendship will exist between both countries and their peoples. The Parties will continue to develop and strengthen their relations on the basis of the principles of respect for sovereignty, territorial integrity, non-interference in each other's internal affairs, and equality. They will cooperate in every possible way in ensuring conditions for the preservation and deepening of the socio-economic gains of their peoples.

Article 2.

The Union of Soviet Socialist Republics and the Somali Democratic Republic will continue to expand and deepen all-round cooperation and the exchange of experience in the economic, scientific and technical fields – industry, land and animal husbandry, irrigation and water conservancy, the development of natural resources, power engineering, the training of national manpower and in other relevant fields of the economy.

The Parties will expand trade and navigation between them on the basis of the principles of mutual advantage and most-favoured-nation treatment in accordance with the provisions of the trade and payments agreement concluded by the two countries in Moscow on June 2, 1961.

Article 3.

The High Contracting Parties will promote the further cooperation between them in the field of science, art, literature, education, health services, press, radio, cinema, television, tourism, sport, and other fields.

The Parties will promote the expansion of cooperation and direct ties between political and mass organizations of the working people, enterprises, cultural and scientific institutions for the purposes of deeper mutual familiarization with the life, work and achievements of the peoples of both countries.

Article 4.

In the interests of strengthening the defence capacity of the Somali Democratic Republic, the High Contracting Parties will continue to develop cooperation in the military field on the basis of relevant agreements between them. This cooperation will envisage, in particular, assistance in the training of the Somalian military personnel and in the mastering of weapons and equipment delivered to the Somali Democratic Republic for the purposes of enhancing its defence potential.

Article 5.

Pursuing peaceful foreign policy, the Union of Soviet Socialist Republics and the Somali Democratic Republic will continue to promote in every possible way the maintenance of peace, and to work for the relaxation of international tensions, for the settlement of international problems by peaceful means, and for the achievement of general and complete disarmament, above all, nuclear disarmament.

Article 6.

The Union of Soviet Socialist Republics respects the policy of non-alignment, conducted by the Somali Democratic Republic, which is an important factor of the maintenance of international peace and security.

The Somali Democratic Republic respects the peace-loving policy conducted by the Union of Soviet Socialist Republics, which is directed at the strengthening of friendship and cooperation with all peoples.

Article 7.

The High Contracting Parties, guided by the ideals of freedom and equality of all peoples, condemn imperialism and colonialism in all forms and manifestations. They will continue to oppose the forces of imperialism and colonialism and cooperate with each other and other states in supporting the just struggle of peoples for freedom, independence and social progress on the basis of the principle of equality and self-determination of peoples, as it is recorded in the Charter of the United Nations Organization.

Article 8.

The High Contracting Parties, expressing their profound interest in ensuring universal peace and security and attaching great importance to cooperation between them in the international arena for attaining these objectives, shall hold regular consultations and exchange opinion with each other on important international questions.

These consultations and exchanges of opinion shall embrace:

– international issues, including situations which cause tension in different parts of the world, with the aim of contributing to the relaxation of tension, the development of cooperation and the strengthening of security;

– questions which are the subject of multilateral negotiations, including those examined in international organizations and at international conferences;

– questions of political, economic and cultural nature and other issues pertaining to relations between the two countries.

These consultations and exchanges of opinion shall be carried out through meetings between leading statesmen of the Parties, visits of official delegations and special representatives, as well as through diplomatic channels.

Article 9.

Should situations arise posing a threat to peace or violating peace, the High Contracting Parties shall without delay come into contact and consult each other with the aim of removing the emergent threat or restoring peace.

Article 10.

Each High Contracting Party declares that it shall not take part in military alliances or any groupings of states, as well as in actions or undertakings directed against the other Contracting Party.

Article 11.

Each High Contracting Party declares that its obligations under existing international treaties do not contradict the provisions of this Treaty and undertakes not to enter into any international agreements incompatible with it.

Article 12.

This Treaty shall remain in force for twenty years from the day of its entry into force.

Unless either High Contracting Party announces one year prior to the expiration of the aforegoing term its desire to terminate the Treaty, it shall remain in force for successive five-year periods until one of the High Contracting Parties furnishes one year prior to the expiration of a given five-year period a written notification of its intent to terminate the Treaty.

Article 13.

This Treaty shall be subject to ratification and shall enter into force on the day of the exchange of instruments of ratification, which shall be held in Moscow in the near future.

Done at Mogadishu on July 11, 1974, in duplicate, in the Russian and Somali languages, both texts being equally authentic.

For the Union	For the Somali
of Soviet Socialist	Democratic Republic
Republics	MOHAMED
N. V. PODGORNY	SIAD BARRE
	(Pravda, October 30, 1974.)

(*Moscow News*, no. 48, November 30, 1974, Supp.)

Notes

I. Oil: The USSR and the Persian Gulf

1 William L. Blackwell, *The Beginning of Russian Industrialization, 1800–1860*, (Princeton University Press, 1968), p. 62.
2 Harry Schwartz, *Russia's Soviet Economy*, second ed., (Englewood Cliffs, N.J., Prentice Hall Inc., 1960), p. 234; Margaret Miller, *The Economic Development of Russia, 1905–1914*, (London, Frank Cass & Co., 1967), pp. 263–267.
3 The British (and to a lesser extent the French) actually controlled the Menshevik anti-Soviet Trans-Caucasian republics of Georgia and Azerbaijan. Lord Curzon planned to make Batum a free port which would give Persia an outlet to the Black Sea and thus become Persia's principal commercial port. He planned on British control of the Batum–Baku railway and an 'internationalization' of Baku and the oilfields surrounding it. (Lord Curzon to the 'Eastern Committee' of the British War Cabinet, December 2, 1918, in Richard M. Ullman, *Anglo-Soviet Relations, 1917–1921*, Britain and the Russian Civil War, November 1918–February 1920, (Princeton, New Jersey, Princeton University Press, 1968), p. 68.
4 *Petroleum Press Service*, (London, November 1967), p. 414.
5 Anthony C. Sutton, *Western Technology and Soviet Economic Development, 1917 to 1930*, (Hoover Institution, Stanford University, Stanford, California, 1968), p. 16.
6 For development of the Caucasus oil fields with foreign, mainly American, assistance, see: *ibid*, pp. 16–44.
7 Louis Fisher, *Oil Imperialism*, (New York, International Publishers, 1926), pp. 238–239.
8 *Pravda*, October 11, 1952.
9 *Petroleum Press Service*, May 1963, p. 166.
10 The Soviet oil deal with Israel was cancelled by the Soviets in November, 1956 on political grounds. See: M. Domke, 'The Israeli–Soviet Oil Arbitration', *American Journal of International Law*, Vol. 53, no. 4, October 1959, pp. 787–806.
11 Interview with Valentin Shashin, USSR Oil Industry Minister, *New Times*, no. 4, January 27, 1971; *Pravda*, February 14, 1971; Report by L. I. Brezhnev, *ibid*, March 31, 1971; Lecture by V. Shashin at the June 1971 Moscow International Oil Congress, *Moscow News*, no. 24, June 12, 1971; *Petroleum Press Service*, March 1973, p. 87; Moscow Radio, January 1, 1974; *TASS*, February 27, 1974. See also: John P. Hardt, 'West Siberia: The Quest for Energy', *Problems of Communism*, (Washington, D.C.), May–June 1973, pp. 25–36.

12 The cost of transporting Siberian oil to European Russian industrial centres is as high, if not higher, than that of its extraction, which makes total expenses double those of the Volga–Ural oil.

13 The shift to nuclear power stations is only in its infancy and no particular priority is given to it. Such a station was inaugurated in Leningrad at the beginning of 1974. According to TASS (August 16, 1974) it was the 'first of a series of similar superpower stations' and its reactor has an electrical capacity of 1 million kilowatts. Nuclear power stations have also been constructed in East Germany and in Czechoslovakia (the latter has some natural uranium). The COMECON formed a special body, Interatomenergo, to supervise and boost a nuclear programme. It aims to construct 60 nuclear power stations by 1980 with a total capacity of 60,000 mW. By 1990 total nuclear output should be 175,000 mW. (*Financial Times*, January 11, 1974).

14 Boris Rachkov, 'The Russian Stake in the Middle East', *New Middle East*, no. 8, May 1969, pp. 36–37.

15 *Economist*, December 1, 1973, p. 40. 1973 figures from *Ekonomicheskaya Gazeta*, no. 26 (June 24, 1974), p. 21.

16 *Der Spiegel*, (Hamburg), December 17, 1973.

17 B. Rachkov, *Ekonomicheskaya Gazeta*, no. 26 (June 24, 1974), p. 21.

18 *Economist*, December 1, 1973, p. 40.

19 Apart from Rumania, which produces her own oil, the other East European countries' dependence on Soviet oil varies from Czechoslovakia's 99 per cent of total imports, to Hungary's 68 per cent. (*Financial Times*, January 11, 1974.)

20 *Economist*, July 10, 1971, p. 90.

21 *New Times*, no. 40, December 1972, p. 14.

22 TASS, February 27, 1974.

23 *New Times*, no. 49, December 1972, p. 14; *Petroleum Press Service*, August 1972, p. 289; *Neue Züricher Zeitung*, (Zurich), December 1, 1970.

24 *Pravda*, December 26, 1967; Baghdad Radio, December 24, 1967; *Mideast Mirror*, (Beirut), December 30, 1967.

25 Baghdad Radio, June 21, 22, 1960.

26 *Ibid* July 5, 29, 1969; *Pravda*, July 6, 1969.

27 *Middle East Economic Digest*, April 16, 1971, p. 404; *Pravda* April 10, 1972; Moscow Radio, June 8, 9, 1972; *Petroleum Press Service*, September 1972, p. 324.

28 Baghdad Radio, September 20, November 5, 1972.

29 Soviet absorption capacity of Iraqi oil was also limited at that time as they had obligated themselves to buy oil from the British Petroleum fields nationalized by Libya.

30 *Pravda*, March 2, 5, 10, 1973; *Izvestia*, March 4, 1973.

31 Moscow Radio, April 9, 1973.

32 *New Times*, no. 48, November 1973, p. 22. In 1973 Soviet oil imports were 14.7 million metric tons. Total exports – 118.3 million, which leaves net exports of 103.6 tons (*The Petroleum Economist*, August 1974, p. 284).

33 Moscow radio in Arabic, January 11, 15, 1974.

34 Moscow radio in Arabic, January 27, 1974.

35 *Ibid*, December 11, 26, 1973.

36 *Ibid*, January 4, 1974.

37 *Ibid*, January 13, 1974; *Pravda*, February 1, 1974. The 1973 oil crisis came just at the time when the Soviets had committed themselves to buying relatively great quantities of nationalized Libyan and Iraqi oil. Without such

a crisis and an increased demand for oil, the Soviets would have had great difficulties in meeting their obligations.

38 *Pravda*, March 17, 1974; *Izvestia*, January 15, March 2, 1974.

39 *Pravda*, March 17, 23, 1974. The strong Soviet animosity to Western oil companies was influenced in no small degree by their traumatic memories of those companies' activities against Soviet Russia and the Soviet regime in its first years.

40 *Ibid.*

41 *Pravda*, February 16, 1974.

42 Moscow radio in Arabic, January 14, 1974.

43 Boris Rachkov, Reuter, January 16, 1974; Moscow radio, January 17, 1974.

44 *Pravda*, February 8, 12, 14, 1974; *Izvestia*, February 8, 1974; Moscow radio in Arabic, February 10–14, 1974.

45 'The Arab East has no intention of ending the embargo; the Arab struggle against Western oil companies strengthened with the aim of bringing about their nationalization', *Izvestia* wrote (February 24, 1974).

46 The 'Peace and Progress' radio station began its Arab language broadcasts in February 1974.

47 Moscow Radio 'Peace and Progress' in Arabic, February 20, 21, 1974.

48 *Ibid*, March 7, 1974.

49 *Ibid*, March 9, 1974; Moscow radio in Arabic, March 11, 12, 14, 1974.

50 Moscow radio in Arabic, March 14, 1974.

51 *Ibid*, March 19, 21, 1974; Radio 'Peace and Progress' in Arabic, March 28, 1974.

52 Jean Heller, AP, April 1, 1974.

II. Russia and the Middle East

1 Frederick Jackson Turner, *The Frontier in American History*, (N.Y., 1920); Donald W. Treadgold, 'Russian Expansion in the light of Turner's Study of the American Frontier', *Agricultural History*, XXVI, October 1952, pp. 147–152.

2 Deputy Foreign Minister A. N. Saltykov to the Commander-in-Chief of Russian forces in the Caucasus line and Gruzia, T. U. Gudovich, January 30 (February 11) 1809, in: USSR, Ministry of Foreign Affairs, *Vneshnaya Polityka Rossii XIX i nachala XX Vyeka* (Russian Foreign Policy in the 19th and beginning of 20th cent.), (Moscow, 1965), Series 1, vol. 4, p. 489.

3 Charles Marvin, *The Russians at the Gates of Herat*, (N.Y., Charles Scribner's Sons, 1885); Seymour Becker, *Russia's Protectorates in Central Asia; Bukhara and Khiva, 1865–1924*, (Harvard University Press, Cambridge, Mass., 1968); Richard A. Pierce, *Russian Central Asia, 1867–1917* (Berkeley, 1960).

4 F. J. Tyutchev, a poet and former diplomat, writing at the end of the 1840s on 'Russian Geography' saw Russia's future frontiers 'from the Nile to Neva, from the Elba to China, from the Volga to the Euphrates, from the Ganges to the Danube'. (F. J. Tyutchev, *Polnoe Sobrainie Stikhotvorenii*, Leningrad, 1957, part 2, pp. 263–264.)

5 Firuz Kazemzadeh, 'The Origin and Early Development of the Persian Cossack Brigade', *The American Slavic and East European Review*, (Seattle) October 1956, pp. 351–363.

6 '*Anglo-Russkow sopernichestvo v Persii 1890–1906 godov*' (Anglo-Russian rivalry in Persia in 1890–1906), *Krasnyi Arkhiv*, (Moscow), 1933, no. 1 (56), p. 46.

7   Ravinder Kumar, *India and the Persian Gulf, 1858–1909*, (London 1965), pp. 141–150.

8   Edward Mead Earle, *Turkey, The Great Powers and the Baghdad Railway*, A study in Imperialism (N.Y., 1935).

9   *Times*, (London), December 1, 1899.

10 *Ibid*, January 12, 1902, giving the views of the Russian Finance Ministry's *Financial Messenger*.

11 *'Tsarskaya Diplomatiya o Zadachakh Rossii na Vostoke v 1900 godu'* (The Tsarist Diplomacy on Russia's Tasks in the East in 1900), *Krasnyi Arkhiv*, 1926, no. 5 (18), pp. 11–13, 17, 19.

12 A. W. Ward and G. P. Gooch, editors, *The Cambridge History British Foreign Policy*, vol. 3, 1866–1919 (X.Y., Macmillan, 1922–1923), p. 320.

13 For the first Russian incursions in the Persian Gulf area and British reactions to them, see: Firuz Kazemzadeh, *Russia and Britain in Persia, 1869–1914. A Study in Imperialism* (Yale University Press, New Haven and London, 1968); Ravinder Kumar, *India and the Persian Gulf Region, 1859–1907*, (London 1965), pp. 216–239.

14 *'K Istorii Anglo-Ruskovo Soglasheniya 1907 goda'* (To the History of the 1907 Anglo-Russian Convention), *Krasnyi Arkhiv*, 1935, nos. 2–3 (69–70), pp. 3–39; R. P. Churchill, *The Anglo-Russian Convention of 1907*, (Iowa, 1939). For part of the convention relating to Persia see: J. C. Hurewitz, *Diplomacy in the Near and Middle East*, vol. 1 (Princeton, D. van Nostrand Co. 1956), pp. 266–267.

III. Soviet Regime – First Stages (1917–1947)

1   The Bolshevik revolution took place according to the Julian calendar on October 25, 1917 and was therefore named the 'October revolution'. That calendar was replaced in February 1918 by the Gregorian one.

2   One of the first steps of the new regime was to publish the Tsarist government's secret agreements. All claims of the old regime to Persia and Turkey were renounced.

3   For Soviet Russia's relations in the first years with Iran and Afghanistan see: Harish Kapur, *Soviet Russia and Asia, 1917–1927*, (Geneva, 1966), pp. 143–241.

4   Konstantin Troyanovski, *Vostok I Revolutsya* (The East and the Revolution), (Moscow, 1918), pp. 47–48.

5   L. Shapiro, *Soviet Treaty Series*. A collection of Bilateral Treaties, Agreements and Conventions etc., concluded between the Soviet Union and Foreign Powers. Vol. 1, 1917–1928, (Washington, D.C., Georgetown University Press, 1950), pp. 93–94.

6   The first Soviet Agent and Consul-General, K. A. Khakimov, a Muslim, presented his credentials to King Hussayn on August 9, 1924. A Hejazi representative arrived in Moscow two months later. (USSR, Ministry of Foreign Affairs, *SSSR i Arabskie Strany, 1917–1960 gody, Dokumenty i Meteryaly*, (The USSR and Arab Countries, 1917–1960, Documents and Materials), (Moscow 1961), pp. 60, 797.)

7   *Ibid*, pp. 61–64, 77–80, 797–798; A. Y. Yoffe, *'Nachaliny etap vzaimootnosheniy Sovetskovo Soyuza z Arabskimi i Afrikanskimi Stranami (1923–1932 goda)'*, (The initial stage of mutual relations of the Soviet Union with Arab and African countries, 1923–1932), *Narody Azii i Afriki*, no. 6, 1965, pp. 57–66; *Mizan*, vol. 8, no. 2, March–April 1966, pp. 87–91. See also: Stephen

Page, *The USSR and Arabia*, (London, Central Asian Research Centre in Association with the Canadian Institute of International Affairs, 1971), pp. 13–24.

8 A letter of Imam Yahya to the Chairman of the USSR Executive Committee (President) M. I. Kalinin of February 25, 1931 indicates satisfaction at the choice of a doctor who became popular as a liaison between Soviets and Arabs. (*SSSR i Arabskie Strany*, loc. cit., pp. 64–77, 798; Yoffe, *ibid*.) The Soviet–Yemeni treaty was extended in 1939 for ten more years.

9 A Soviet trade representative visited Eritrea for three years beginning in 1931. At the same time a Soviet–Ethiopian agreement was signed providing for a supply of Soviet oil products. No diplomatic relations were established between the two countries. (Yoffe, *ibid*.)

10 Raymond J. Sontag and James S. Beddie, eds., *Nazi–Soviet Relations, 1939–1941*, Documents from the Archives of the German Foreign Office (Washington, Department of State, 1948), pp. 242–243, 247–254.

11 *Ibid*, p. 257.

12 *Ibid*, pp 258–259. Two other conditions related to Finland and Japan.

13 *Ibid*, pp. 260–264. A great number of Western history books that deal with that period describe in detail the parts of those German–Soviet negotiations that deal with the Middle East, but most of them describe the German proposals as though they were Soviet ones, ignoring the unsuccessful German attempts to distract Soviet attention from Europe to the Middle East.

14 T. H. Vail Motter, *The Persian Corridor and Aid to Russia*, (U.S. Department of the Army, Office of Military History, US Army in World War II, the Middle East Theater, Washington, D.C. 1952), p. 545.

15 James F. Byrness, *Speaking Frankly*, (London, Heinemann, 1947), pp. 94–96; H. Feis, *Between War and Peace: The Potsdam Conference*, (London, Oxford University Press, 1960), pp. 307–309; *Foreign Relations of the United States*, Diplomatic Papers, The Conference of Berlin (The Potsdam Conference), 1945, vol. 2 (Washington, D.C., US Government Printing Office, 1960).

16 For Soviet demands see: *Foreign Affairs*, (N.Y.), April 1949, pp. 458–459; Harry S. Truman, *Memoirs*, vol. 1, 1945, *Year of Decisions*, (N.Y. 1955), pp. 413–415, 424–426.

IV. Limited Soviet Successes (1940–late 1950s)

1 Such Soviet demands were presented, inter alia, by Foreign Minister Molotov on June 7, 1945. For Soviet demands see: *Foreign Affairs* (N.Y.), April 1949, pp. 458–459; Harry S. Truman, *Memoirs*, vol. 1, 1945: *Year of Decisions*, (N.Y. 1955), pp. 413–414, 424–426.

2 President Harry S. Truman's message to US Congress, March 12, 1947. *Department of State Bulletin*, vol. 16, supplement, May 4, 1947, pp. 829–832.

3 Sepher Zadik, 'Communism in Iran', *Problems of Communism*, vol. 14, no. 5, September–October 1965, pp. 46–55.

4 For the changes that appeared in Soviet appraisal of Afro-Asian states see: Aryeh Yodfat, *Arab Politics in the Soviet Mirror*, (Israel University Press, Jerusalem, 1973); Jaan Pennar, *The USSR and the Arabs, the Ideological Dimension*, (C. Hurst and Co., London, 1973).

5 U.S. Department of State Publications no. 6446, *Foreign Policy 1950–1955, Basic Documents*, vol. 1, pp. 1257–1259.

6 For the Soviet–Egyptian arms deal and its background, see: Uri Ra'anan,

The USSR Arms the Third World, (Cambridge, Mass. and London, 1969), pp. 13–172.

7 *Mideast Mirror*, (Cairo), November 19, 1955, p. 6.

8 For Soviet writings on Arabian Peninsula countries, see: Stephen Page, *The USSR and Arabia*, (London, Central Asian Research Centre in association with the Canadian Institute of International Affairs, 1971).

9 *Vedomosti Verkhovnovo Sovieta SSSR*, no. 8 (850), April 20, 1956.

10 *Pravda*, March 10, 1956.

11 According to the *New York Times* (March 3, 1957), Yemen received arms from Czechoslovakia after a refusal from Western countries to supply them. There is, however, evidence that Soviet arms had already arrived there in 1956.

12 *Izvestia*, June 23 and 24, 1956.

13 *Mideast Mirror*, April 5, 1959, p. 8; U.S. Department of State, *Communist Economic Policy in the Less Developed Areas*, (Washington, 1960), p. 27; Department of State, Bureau of Intelligence and Research, *The Sino–Soviet Economic Offensive Through 1960*, (Washington, 1961), p. 9; *Ibid, 1962*, p. 30.

14 US Department of State, *United States Policy in the Middle East, September 1956–June 1957*, (Washington, D.C., August 1957), pp. 23–24.

15 Describing the Soviet position on Arab unity, *Pravda* (April 14, 1963) wrote: 'It all depends on who carries the banner of unity and on what basis it will be realized – anti-imperialist, democratic, popular, or pro-imperialist and anti-democratic.'

16 *Izvestia*, July 17 and 19, 1958.

17 *Pravda*, October 13, 1958; *Vedomosti Verkhovnovo Sovieta SSSR*, April 23 and November 26, 1959.

18 In July 1958 Nasser visited Moscow. According to Hassanayn Haykal in *Al-Ahram* (Cairo, January 22, 1965) Khrushchev told him: "The USSR is not ready for a confrontation with the West, the results of which are not certain . . . we will provide you with all the means of political support. . . . We can announce that the USSR will arrange large scale military exercises on its southern front. . . . I am not worried that the West will consider us prepared for more than exercises, but I am worried that you yourself may believe there is more in it.'

19 For Soviet views on Iraq's internal and inter-Arab policies from the 1958 revolution until the end of the 1960s, see: Aryeh Yodfat, *Arab Politics in the Soviet Mirror*, (Israel University Press, 1973). For Iraqi communist positions and Iraqi politics in general, see: Uriel Dann, *Iraq Under Qassem: A Political History, 1958–1963*, (N.Y., Praeger, 1963); Majid Khadduri, *Republican Iraq: A Study of Iraqi Politics Since the Revolution of 1958*, (London, Oxford University Press, 1969).

20 An Iraqi communist's 'self-criticism' was published in the ICP's *Ittihad ash-Sha'ab*, (August 3, 1959), and in the CPSU ideological organ *Komunist* (no. 12, August 1959, pp. 104–109). The subsequent events in 1971 in Sudan, where such an attempt was made but failed, seems to justify the Soviet position of that time.

V. The Breakthrough (late 1950s–1967)

1 G. J. Pyasetski, *Na Postynnom Beregu Tihamy* (On the Desert Coast of the Tihama), (Moscow, 1967). In 1958–1961 the author was head of a group of Soviet experts who built the port of Hudayda.

2   *Pravda*, October 2, 1962.
3   *Pravda*, March 25, 1964.
4   US Department of State. Bureau of Intelligence and Research, *The Communist Economic Offensive Through 1964*, (RSB-65, August 4, 1965), p. 14; *Asian Affairs*, April 1966, p. 224.
5   Jidda radio, August 9, 1967. At the Khartoum Arab Summit Conference in August, Egypt had undertaken to withdraw its forces from Yemen. However, said a Soviet commentator, the Khartoum agreement would not affect Yemen's internal political situation, (*Pravda*, September 1, 1967).
6   *Fatat al-Gezirah*, (Aden), October 7, 1967.
7   Cairo radio, Aden radio, November 18, 1967; *Mideast Mirror*, November 25, 1967, p. 16.
8   *Al-Hawadith*, (Beirut), December 15, 1967; *New York Times*, December 14 and 15, 1967. A royalist broadcast stated on December 3, 1967, that their anti-aircraft guns had shot down near San'a a Tupolev plane together with its Soviet pilot engaged in raiding royalist positions. *Al-Hayat*, November 9, 1968. On October 23, 1968 a royalist broadcast claimed that several Soviet experts were killed during a battle.
9   Soviet military involvement in Yemen at the time was greatly exaggerated by Arab and some Western papers.
10 Cairo radio, May 20, 1964.
11 *Pravda*, May 25, 1964.
12 *Izvestia*, November 29, 1964.
13 *U.S. News and World Report*, April 23, 1962.
14 According to the London *Economist* (July 21, 1962), the US cut off its military aid to Iran.
15 *Pravda*, September 17, 1962.
16 V. Lednev, *Izvestia*, December 19, 1962.
17 *New York Times*, July 14, 1966.
18 *Le Monde*, February 21, 1967.

VI. Anticipating a Vacuum in the Gulf (1967–1971)

1   Parliamentary Debates, House of Commons, vol. 756. col. 1580.
2   *Pravda*, January 20, 1968.
3   Geoffrey Jukes, 'The Indian Ocean in Soviet Naval Policy' (London, International Institute for Strategic Studies, *Adelphi Papers*, no. 87, May 1972); Mordechai Abir, 'Red Sea Politics', *Adelphi Papers*, no. 93, December 1972.
4   *Pravda*, January 24, 1968; World Marxist Review, vol. II, no. 7, (July 1968), p. 48.
5   K. Ivanov, 'Saudi Double-Dealing', *New Times*, no. 8, February 28, 1968, pp. 16–18.
6   *Pravda*, September 6, 1969.
7   *New Times*, no. 39, September 30, 1969, p. 22.
8   *New Times*, no. 52, December 30, 1969, pp. 26–30.
9   *Pravda*, July 17, 1968; G. Drambyants, *New Times*, no. 11, March 19, 1969, p. 19.
10 *Pravda*, February 28, 1968.
11 Beirut's *As-Safa* (April 3, 1968) declared that Soviet support of Iran was tantamount to taking sides with a non-Arab country against the Arabs.
12 *Pravda*, March 4, 1968.

13 Qatar proclaimed its independence in early September 1971. Recognition was granted by the USSR by telegram on September 10, (*Izvestia*, September 12, 1971). Recognition was granted by China the same day (NCNA, September 10, 1971). Neither the telegrams nor their replies mentioned diplomatic relations and no such relations were established.

14 *Izvestia*, August 17, 1971.

15 Soviet media described the year 1958 as the beginning of the 'Dhufar Liberation Front', without distinguishing between the Dhufar rebellion, which began in the 1960s and the rebellion of Imam Ghalib or Jabal Akhdar, which was in fact a part of the long-standing clash between the Ibadhi Imamate, encouraged by Saudi Arabia, and the Sultan of Oman. See: Mordechai Abir, *Oil Power & Politics*, (London, Frank Cass, 1974), pp. 14–15. See also: 'A new liberation front', *New Times*, no. 1, January 1, 1969, p. 25. For further involvement of the USSR with PFLOAG see below.

16 Chou En-Lai's message to the Emir of Bahrayn on August 20, 1971 announced Chinese recognition (NCNA, August 20, 1971). A similar telegram was sent from USSR's President Podgorny to the Emir on August 25 (TASS).

17 Amirie Abbas: *The Persian Gulf and Indian Ocean in International Politics*, Teheran, 1975, pp. 294–5.

VII. 'In the Direction of the Persian Gulf' (1972–1975)

1 *Pravda*, April 11, 1972.

2 *Pravda*, February 12, 1972.

3 For full text, see appendix.

4 This clause was similar to the Soviet–Egyptian agreement and the one with India.

5 *The Times* (London), April 6, 1972.

6 *Pravda*, September 20, 1972.

7 See below. The province of Khusistan in western Iran contains a high proportion of Arabs among its population. See also: Mordechai Abir, *Oil, Power & Politics*, p. 32.

8 *Sotsialisticheskaya Industriya*, September 16, 1972.

9 *Ibid*, January 9, 1973.

10 *Al-Nahar*, February 17, March 11, 1972; *Al-Hayat*, February 17, April 25, 1972.

11 Mordechai Abir, 'The Role of the Persian Gulf Oil in Middle Eastern and International Relations', *Jerusalem Papers Series*, Leonard Davis Institute for International Relations, Hebrew University, Jerusalem, 1976.

12 Social injustice and stratification in Kuwait, according to Soviet sources, would lead to a social and political explosion. See: A. Vasilyev, *Pravda*, October 10, 1972.

13 For Shahbahar – *Jerusalem Post*, January 9, 1973. For activity in Oman – *Financial Times*, 30, 31 January 1973; *Al-Siyassah* (Kuwait), January 8, 1974.

14 Moscow radio in Persian, July 14, 1972; TASS, July 22, 1972.

15 *Pravda*, March 18, 1973.

16 *L'Orient le Jour*, March 21, 1973.

17 By the end of 1973 the USSR supplied Iraq with $724 million worth of arms. See: US Arms Control and Disarmament Agency, *World Military Expenditures, 1963–1973*, (Washington 1975), p. 70.

18 Because of Soviet insistence in the course of the October 1973 War, Algeria's president Boumedienne gave Moscow a cheque for $2 billion for arms supplied to Egypt.
19 See below chapter X: Power Rivalry in the Indian Ocean, p. 124.
20 See visit of Supreme Soviet delegation to Kuwait in March 1974 and articles such as *Izvestia* (March 19, 1974); Radio Moscow in Arabic, March 19, 1974. On lower Gulf see: A. Vasilyev, *Pravda*, May 31, 1974.
21 *An-Nida* (Beirut), December 30, 1973; Radio Moscow in Arabic, January 8, February 10, 12, 1974.
22 Radio Moscow in Arabic, February 12, 1974.
23 At the beginning of 1974 a Kuwaiti delegation visited the USSR to purchase modern weapons. See: *Tanjug* (Belgrade), January 31, 1974. After lengthy negotiations the Kuwaitis ordered the latest modern weapons, but they opted for Syrian, not Soviet instructors – DAFA May 16, 1976.
24 Increasing Saudi pressure on the PDRY and PFLOAG in 1972 and early 1973 occasioned the attacks on Saudi Arabia in the Soviet foreign affairs weekly *New Times* – D. Voilsky, 'King Faisal's "Holy War" ', *New Times*, no. 5, February 1973, pp. 26–27.
25 Moscow radio in Arabic, February 20, 1973.
26 Moscow radio (Moscow radio in Arabic, November 13, 1973) stated that it was the first time such greetings had been sent by the Saudi monarch. See also: *Izvestia*, November 14, 1973.
27 *Izvestia*, December 4, 1973.
28 In addition to the possibility of establishing diplomatic ties there were claims that King Faysal had accepted an invitation to visit Moscow – *Al-Nahar* (Beirut), November 19, 1973. According to the Kuwaiti *As-Siyassah* (December 2, 1973), King Faysal planned to visit the USSR or a Soviet personality was planning to visit Saudi Arabia – *Al-Muharir* (Beirut), December 5, 1973.
29 *Al-Nahar*, April 3, 1974; Moscow radio 'Peace and Progress' in Arabic, April 4, 1974.
30 Moscow radio broadcasts in September 1974 once more reiterated the potential benefits and advantages of relations with the Soviet Union.
31 *Ettelaat* (Teheran), May 26, 1974. A *Pravda* article by A. Vasilyev published a few days later (May 31) stated that gas from Kuwait, Saudi Arabia, Qatar and Iraq was being burnt and wasted, hinting that if the USSR did not buy Iran's gas the same would happen. In conclusion, Iran's role in the Gulf and her immense purchases of arms in the West were criticized. The article brought sharp reactions from the Iranian press. In August a compromise was reached according to which the price of Iranian gas exported to the USSR was raised from 30 to 57 cents per 1,000 cubit feet – Teheran radio, August 17, 1974.
32 Large shipments of sophisticated Soviet arms such as Mig 23s and SCUD SSMs to Iraq continued during 1974 – Dale Tahtinen, *Arms in the Persian Gulf* (American Enterprise Institute, Washington 1974).
33 *Foreign Broadcasting Information Service*, December 4, 1974, Riyadh, December 3, 1974.
34 *FT*. March 20, 1975; *Al-Quds* (Israel); March 10, 1975.
35 At the same time they gave their blessing to a similar process between the PDRY and Saudi Arabia and its allies in the Gulf. See below.
36 For Iraqi economic relations with the United States see: *FT*, July 30, 1975.
37 *Jerusalem Post*, May 12, 1975; *Al-Sayyad* (Beirut); May 29, 1975.
38 On Prince Fahd's visit to Iraq – *FT*, June 1, 1975. Agreements between

Riyadh and Baghdad, MENA, Cairo, July 2, 1975; *Ma'ariv* (Israel), July 3, 1975. Tension in Iraqi–Soviet relations – *Ha'aretz* (Israel), July 11, 1975.

39 *Ash-Sha'ab* (Jerusalem), March 2, 1975; *Al-Hadaf* (Beirut), May 10, 1975; *International Herald Tribune*, May 28, 1975; *Al-Sayyad*, July 3, 1975. Since August 1975 many items appeared in the Arab press concerning the suppression of trade unions, leftist movements and personal liberties in Bahrayn, possibly in alliance with Riyadh.

40 For renewal of the basing agreement with Bahrayn – *Al-Sayyad*, January 16–23, 1975. For Sultan Qabus' visit to US and cooperation with Americans, *Al-Hadaf*, March 1, 1975. Bahrayn's request to terminate the basing agreement – *Al-Ra'i al-'Amm* (Kuwait), November 11, 1975. American fleets in the Gulf area – *Al-Ra'i al-'Amm*, October 28, 1975.

41 *IHT* (July 29, 1976) on the Gorshkov doctrine.

VIII. South Yemen – The Cuba of the Middle East

1 Abir, *Oil*, chapter II: Crisis in Southern Arabia.

2 *Izvestia*, December 3, 1967.

3 *Pravda*, February 10, 1969.

4 *NY Times*, June 25, 1969.

5 At the end of 1969 relations between the PRSY and Saudi Arabia degenerated into a limited war. It was alleged that a Soviet colonel commanded the PRSY Air Force and that he flew one of the seven Mig-17 jets which took part in the skirmishes, while Soviet military advisers commanded the PRSY ground forces. (*Sunday Telegraph*, December 7, 1969.)

6 Eric Rouleau, *Le Monde*, May 31, 1972.

7 Aden radio, June 3, 1970.

8 Joint communiqué issued on the visit, *Pravda*, November 26, 1972.

9 *The Times*, January 2, 1971; *Sunday Times*, February 7, 1971; *NY Times*, March 14, 1971.

10 By May 1972 the PDRY had received, in addition to various artillery pieces, over 50 T-34 tanks, 20 Mig-17s and Mig-19s, fighter interceptors, several transport bombers, helicopters and a number of small patrol boats. Unconfirmed reports claimed that the PDRY was given a squadron of Mig-21s and other more sophisticated weapons. (*Daily Telegraph*, May 9, 1972.)

11 According to exiled South Yemen former Prime Minister 'Abd al-Qawi Makkawi, more than 600 Soviet experts went to Aden after their services in Egypt were terminated in July 1972, and they were still there in early 1973. (*Al-Jaridah* (Beirut), February 2, 1973.

12 According to President Ruba'i 'Ali (*Al Ahram* (Egypt), September 11, 1974), 'the Soviets have no permanent presence in any port of the PDRY . . . the facilities granted to them in Aden do not exceed the facilities given to any other party'.

13 As the Soviets publish nothing about their military involvement in foreign countries, our information on this matter comes mainly from Arab and Western sources. See for instance: *Daily Telegraph*, July 23, 1973.

14 *Le Monde*, February 10, 1972, quoting the Economic Adviser of the USSR embassy in Aden.

15 *Pravda*, March 9, 1973; Aden radio, March 13, 1973.

16 Baghdad radio, September 7, 1973.

17   See for instance: *Al-Anwar*, (Beirut), February 2, 1975; *Al-Quds*, (Jerusalem), February 27, 1975.
18   Regarding the Arab solidarity line of Ruba'i 'Ali, see: *Al-Jadid* (Beirut), September 20, 1974. On cooperation with Arab countries – *Al-'Usbu al-'Arabi* (Beirut), May 19, 1975; *Al-Hurriyah* (Beirut), June 30, 1975.
19   *The Economist* (London, September 14, 1974), reported the probable erasure of a $15 million debt owed by South Yemen to the USSR. Other sources reported Soviet cancellation of a $50 million PDRY debt. For Arab aid see, MENA (Cairo), November 11, 1975; *Al-Diyar* (Beirut), November 12, 1975; *Al-Ahram*, November 29, 1975; *IHT*, May 28, 1975.
20   MENA, November 27, 1975; ANA, November 23, 1975. For the UAE's aid to the PDRY see: *FT*, July 1, 1975.

IX. Power Rivalry in the Indian Ocean

1   See, for instance: *The Defense Monitor*, Center for Defense Information, Washington, vol. 3, no. 3, April 1974; S. Karnow, *New Republic*, May 4, 1974.
2   *Adelphi Papers* (IISS, London), no. 87, May 1972.
3   'Conflicts in Africa', *Adelphi Papers*, (ISS, London), no. 93, December 1972, pp. 25–41.
4   Very illuminating facts about the Soviet strategic infrastructure and naval power in the Indian Ocean were published in a United Nations document which was later 'withdrawn' under pressure from the USSR and its allies in the region (United Nations General Assembly, A/AC/159/1, May 3, 1974). The document also deals with American activity in the region. See also US Secretary of Defence Schlesinger's exposé of the stockpiling of missiles in and the character of the Soviet base in Berbera, July/August 1975.
5   Radio Moscow, July 22, 1976.
6   *Wall Street Journal*, July 1, 1975.
7   For a greatly exaggerated evaluation of Chinese interests in the Indian Ocean see: H. Laboussse, *Le Golfe et le Canal*, Paris 1973.
8   For Soviet naval theory and peacetime use of navies see: The Gorshkov Papers by E. T. Wooldridge, *ORBIS*, Winter 1975, pp. 1153–1175.
9   S. Karnow, 'Confrontation in the Gulf', *New Republic*, May 4, 1974.
10   *Daily Express*, April 2, 1974; *FT*, April 14, 1974, May 15, 1974; J. C. Campbell, 'The Super Powers and the Persian Gulf' in Abbas Amirie (ed.), *The Persian Gulf and the Indian Ocean*, Teheran 1975.
11   Evans and Novak quoting from a new book by Admiral Sergei Gorshkov – *IHT*, July 29, 1976.
12   The Gorshkov concept, – *IHT*, July 29, 1976.

Bibliography

BOOKS

Abir, Mordechai. 1974. *Oil, power and politics. Conflict in Arabia, the Red Sea and the Gulf*. London: Frank Cass.

Agwani, Mohammed Shafi. 1968. *Communism in the Arab east*. London: Asia Publishing House.

Allen, Robert Loring. 1958. *Middle Eastern economic relations with the Soviet Union, eastern Europe and mainland China*. Charlottesville, Virginia: University of Virginia.

Amirie, Abbas (ed.). 1975. *The Persian Gulf and the Indian Ocean in international politics*. Teheran: IIPES.

Bloomfield, Lincoln P., and Leiss, Amelia C. 1969. *Controlling small wars: A strategy for the 1970s*. New York: Alfred A. Knopf.

Bodyanskiy, V. L. 1962. *Bakhreyn* (Bahrain). Moscow: Jedatelstvo Vostochnoy Literatura.

—, and Lazarev, M. S. 1967. *Saudovskaya Araviya posle Sauda* (Saudi Arabia after Saud). Moscow: Nauka.

Burrell, R. M. 1972. *The Persian Gulf*. Washington, D.C.: Center for Strategic and International Studies, Georgetown University.

—, and Cottrell, Alvin J. 1972. *Iran, the Arabian peninsula and the Indian Ocean*. New York: National Strategy Information Center.

Campbell, John C. 1960. *Defense of the Middle East: Problems of American policy*. New York: Harper and Brothers.

Center for Strategic and International Studies. 1969. *The Gulf: Implications of British withdrawal*. Washington, D.C.: Georgetown University.

Cottrell, Alvin J., and Burrell, R. M. 1971. *The Indian Ocean: A conference report*. Washington, D.C.: Center for Strategic and International Studies.

— —. 1972. *The Indian Ocean: Its political, economic and military importance*. New York: Praeger.

Curzon, George N. 1966 (First edition, 1892). *Persia and the Persian Gulf question*. London: Frank Cass & Co.

Dallin, David J. 1962. *Soviet foreign policy after Stalin*. London: Methuen & Co.

Dann, Uriel. 1969. *Iraq under Qassem*. Jerusalem: Israel Universities Press.

Dlin, N. A., and Zvereva, L. S. 1968. *Kuweyt* (Kuwait). Moscow: Mysl.

Drambyatnts, G. G. 1968. *Persidsky Zaliv bez Romantiki* (The Persian Gulf without romantics). Moscow: Mezhdunavaelynyye Otnesheniya.

Ebel, Robert E. 1970. *Communist trade in oil and gas*. New York: Praeger.

Eudin, Henia, and North, Robert S. 1957. *Soviet Russia and the east, 1920–1927. A documentary survey*. Stanford, California: Stanford University Press.

Evolution of communism in Iran. 1959. Teheran: Kayhan Press.

Fisher, Louis. 1926. *Oil imperialism*. New York: International Publishers.

Freedman, Robert O. 1975. *Soviet policy toward the Middle East since 1970.* New York: Praeger.

Gerasimov, O., and Mashin, Yu. 1966. *V Gorakh Yuzhnoy Aravii* (In the mountains of South Arabia). Moscow: Mysl.

Golubovskaya, E. 1965. *Yemen.* Moscow: Mysl.

Hunter, Robert E. 1969. *The Soviet dilemma in the Middle East.* London: Institute for Strategic Studies: Adelphi Papers Nos. 59 and 60.

Hurewitz, Jacob C. 1956. *Diplomacy in the Near and Middle East: A documentary record.* 2 Vols. Princeton: Van Nostrand.

—. 1969. *Soviet-American rivalry in the Middle East.* New York: Praeger.

Jukes, Geoffrey. 1972. *The Indian Ocean in Soviet naval policy.* London: The International Institute for Strategic Studies: Adelphi Papers No. 87.

Kaushik, Devendra. 1972. *The Indian Ocean.* Delhi: Vilzas Publications.

Khadduri, Majid. 1969. *Republican Iraq.* London: Oxford University Press.

Landis, Lincoln. 1973. *Politics and oil: Moscow in the Middle East.* London, New York: Dunella.

Laqueur, Walter. 1969. *The struggle for the Middle East.* London: Routledge and Kegan Paul.

—. 1959. *The Soviet Union and the Middle East.* London: Routledge and Kegan Paul.

Lenczowski, George. 1949. *Russia and the west in Iran, 1918–1948: A study in big-power rivalry.* Cornell University Press.

—. 1972. *Soviet advances in the Middle East.* Washington, D.C.: American Enterprise Institute for Public Policy Research.

Little, T. 1968. *South Arabia: Arena of conflict.* London: Pall Mall.

Macro, E. 1968. *Yemen and the western world.* London: C. Hurst.

McLane, Charles B. 1973. *Soviet Middle East relations.* London: Central Asian Research Centre, and New York: Columbia University Press.

Medvedko, L. J. 1973. *Vyetry peremen V Persidskom Zalive* (Winds of changes in the Persian Gulf). Moscow.

Monroe, Elizabeth Rapportense. 1973. *The changing balance of power in the Persian Gulf.* New York: American Universities Field Staff.

O'Ballance, Edgar. 1971. *The war in the Yemen.* London: Faber and Faber.

Odell, Peter R. 1974. *Oil and world power: Background to the oil crisis.* New York: Penguin, 3rd Edition.

Ozoling, V. 1968. *Saudovskaya Araviya* (Saudi Arabia). Moscow: Mysl.

Page, Stephen. 1971. *The USSR and Arabia.* London: Central Asian Research Centre.

Pennar, Jaan. 1973. *The USSR and the Arabs: The ideological dimension.* New York: Crane, Russak.

Price, D. L. 1975. *Oman: Insurgency and development.* London: Conflict Studies No. 53, January 1975.

Ra'anan, Uri. 1969. *The USSR arms the Third World.* Cambridge, Massachusetts: The M.I.T. Press.

Ramazani, Rouhollah K. 1972. *The Persian Gulf: Iran's role.* Charlottesville, Virginia: University Press of Virginia.

Rawlinson, Henry. 1970. *England and Russia in the east.* New York: Praeger. First edition 1875.

The security of the Cape oil route. 1974. London: Report of a study group of the Institute for the Study of Conflict.

Schapiro, Leonard, ed. 1950–55. *Soviet treaty series: A collection of bilateral agreements and conventions etc., concluded between the Soviet Union and foreign powers.* Washington, D.C.: Georgetown University Press. 2 Volumes.

Schmidt, Dana Adams. 1968. *Yemen: The unknown war*. New York: Holt, Rinehart and Winston.

Shvakov, A. V. 1969. *Probuzhdeniye Aravii* (The awakening of Arabia). Moscow: Mezhdunavadnyye Otnosheniya.

Sinolansky, Oles M. 1974. *The Soviet Union and the Arab east under Khrushchev*. Lewisburg, Pennsylvania: Bucknell University Press.

Soviet objectives in the Middle East. 1974. London: Report of a study group of the Institute for the Study of Conflict.

Spector, Ivan. 1959. *The Soviet Union and the Muslim world, 1917–1958*. Seattle: University of Washington Press.

Tahtinen, Dale R. 1974. *Arms in the Persian Gulf*. Washington, D.C.: American Enterprise Institute for Public Research.

U.S. Congress, 93rd Conference, 2nd Session. 1975. *The Persian Gulf, 1974; Money, politics, arms and power*. Hearings before the Subcommittee on Foreign Affairs, House of Representatives, July–August 1974. Washington: Government Printing Office.

USSR Academy of Sciences, Institute of Ethnography. 1970. *Natsyonalniye Protsesy v Stranakh Blizhnevo i Svednevo Vostoka* (National processes in the Near and Middle East countries). Moscow: Nauka.

USSR, Ministry of Foreign Affairs. 1961. *SSSR i Arabskiye Strany, 1917–1960: Dokumenty i Materialy* (USSR and Arab countries, 1917–1960: Documents and materials). Moscow: Izdatel'stvo Politicheskoy Literatury.

Wenner, Manfred W. 1967. *Modern Yemen 1918–1966*. Baltimore: Johns Hopkins Press.

Yodfat, Aryeh. 1973. *Arab politics in the Soviet mirror*. New York and Toronto: Halsted Press, John Wiley and Sons.

Zabih, Sepher. 1966. *The communist movement in Iran*. Berkeley and Los Angeles: University of California Press.

ARTICLES

Abir, Mordechai. Red Sea Politics. *Adelphi Papers*, No. 95, International Institute for Strategic Studies, London 1972.

—. Sharm al-Sheikh – Bab al-Mandab: The Strategic Balance and Israel's Southern Approaches. *Jerusalem Papers on Peace Problems*, No. 5. The Leonard Davis Institute for International Relations, The Hebrew University Jerusalem, March 1974.

—. The Role of the Persian Gulf Oil in Middle Eastern and International Relations. *Jerusalem Papers on Peace Problems*, No. 20. The Leonard Davis Institute for International Relations, The Hebrew University Jerusalem, September 1976.

Ballis, William B. 1965. Soviet–Iranian relations during the decade 1953–64. *Bulletin, Institute for the Study of the USSR*. Munich, November 1965, pp. 9–22.

Barger, Thomas C. 1972. Middle Eastern oil since the Second World War. *The Annals of the American Academy of Political and Social Science*. (Hereafter: *The Annals . . .*), May 1972, pp. 31–44.

Berry, John A. 1972. Oil and Soviety policy in the Middle East. *The Middle East Journal*. Washington, D.C., spring 1972. pp. 149–160.

Burrell, R. M. 1972. Rebellion in Dhofar: The spectre of Vietnam. *New Middle East*, London, March–April 1972. pp. 55–58.

Campbell, John C. 1972. The Communist powers and the Middle East: Moscow's purposes. *Problems of Communism.* Washington, D.C., September–October 1972. pp. 40–54.

Campbell, John C. 1972. The Soviet Union and the United States in the Middle East. *The Annals . . .*, May 1972, pp. 126–135.

Chaplin, Dennis. 1975. Somalia and the development of Soviet activity in the Indian Ocean. *Military Affairs* (U.S. Army). July 1975, pp. 3–9.

Cobley, John K. 1975. The shifting sands of Arab communism. *Problems of Communism.* March–April 1975, pp. 22–42.

Gaspard, J. 1969. Faisal's Arabian alternative. *New Middle East.* March 1969, pp. 15–19.

Griffith, William E. 1976. Soviet influence in the Middle East. *Survival.* London, January–February 1976. pp. 2–9.

Halliday, Fred. 1970. Counter-revolution in the Yemen. *New Left Review.* London, September–October 1970, pp. 3–25.

Hardt, John P. 1973. West Siberia: The quest for energy. *Problems of Communism.* May–June 1973, pp. 25–36.

Hottinger, Arnold. 1971. Ferment in the Persian Gulf. *Swiss Review of World Affairs.* Zurich, February 1971, pp. 12–16.

—. 1973. King Faisal, oil and Arab politics. *Swiss Review of World Affairs.* October 1973, pp. 8–10.

—. 1974. The reopening of the Suez Canal. The race for power in the Indian Ocean. *The Round Table.* London, October 1974, pp. 393–402.

Hurewitz, J. C. 1972. The Persian Gulf: British withdrawal and western security. *The Annals . . .*, May 1972, pp. 106–115.

Jukes, Geoffrey. 1971. The Soviet Union and the Indian Ocean. *Survival.* November 1971, pp. 370–375.

Kennedy, Edward M. 1975. The Persian Gulf: Arms race or arms control? *Foreign Affairs.* October 1975, pp. 14–35.

Kimche, Jon. 1974. Soviet oil diplomacy before and after the October war. *Midstream.* New York, December 1974, pp. 5–12.

Luchsinger, Fred. 1973. Rumblings in Araby: The Dhofar rebellion. *Swiss Review of World Affairs.* December 1973, pp. 18–20.

Meister, Jurg. 1974. Diego Garcia: Outpost in the Indian Ocean. *Swiss Review of World Affairs.* April 1974, pp. 6–7.

Rochkov, Boris. 1969. The Russian stake in the Middle East. *The New Middle East.* May 1969, pp. 36–37.

Smolansky, O. M. 1970. Moscow and the Persian Gulf: An analysis of Soviet ambitions and potential. *Orbis.* Philadelphia, Spring 1970, pp. 92–108.

Tekinev, Suleiman. 1969. Soviet–Iranian relations over the last half century. *Studies on the Soviet Union.* Munich, 8(4): pp. 36–44.

Thomas, Roy E. 1973. Iraq and the Persian Gulf region. *Current History.* January 1973, pp. 21–25, 37.

Toole, Wycliffe D. 1968. Soviet interests in Arabia. *Military Review.* May 1968, pp. 91–97.

Tucker, Robert W. 1975. Oil: The issue of American intervention. *Commentary.* New York, January 1975, pp. 21–31.

—. 1975. A new international order. *Commentary.* February 1975, pp. 38–50.

—. 1975. Further reflections on oil and force. *Commentary.* March 1975, pp. 45–56.

Watt, D. C. 1972. The Persian Gulf – Cradle of conflict. *Problems of Communism,* May–June 1972, pp. 32–40

Wheeler, Geoffrey. 1972. The Indian Ocean area: Soviet aims and interests. *Asian Affairs.* London, October 1972, pp. 270–274.

L

Wright, E. M. 1941–2. Iran as a gateway to Russia. *Foreign Affairs* 20, 1941–2, pp. 367–371.

Yapp, M. E. 1976. The Soviet Union and the Middle East. *Asian Affairs*. February 1976, pp. 7–18.

Yodfat, Aryeh. 1969. Unpredictable Iraq poses a Russian problem. *New Middle East*. October 1969, pp. 17–20.

—. 1971. The People's Republic of South Yemen. *New Outlook*. Tel Aviv, March 1971, pp. 43–48.

—. 1971. Russia's other Middle East pasture – Iraq. *New Middle East*. November 1971, pp. 26–29.

—. 1971. The USSR and Arab communist parties. *New Middle East*. May 1971, pp. 29–33.

—. 1975. The Soviet line on Saudi Arabia. *Soviet Analyst*. London, September 18th, 1975, pp. 4–5.

Zabih, Sepher. 1965. Communism in Iran. *Problems of Communism*. September–October 1965, pp. 46–55.

PERIODICALS AND NEWSPAPERS USED

Abbreviations: B – Beirut.   L – London.   M – Moscow.   NY – New York.
K – Kuwait.

Afro-Asian Affairs, L
Al-Ahram, Cairo
Aviation Week, NY
Azia i Afrika Sevodnia, M
Bakinski Rabochy, Baku
Christian Science Monitor, Boston
Daily Report, Foreign Broadcast Information Service (FBIS), USA
Daily Telegraph, L
The Economist, L
Financial Times, L
Guardian, L
Al-Hurriyah, B
Al-Hadaf, B
Al-Hayat, B
Al-Hawadith, B
Al-Muharir, B
An-Nida, B
Al-Ra'i al 'Amm, K
Al-Siyassah, K
Al-Sayyad, B
International Affairs, L
International Affairs, M
International Herald Tribune, Paris
Izvestia, M
Jeune Afrique, Paris
Kayhan, Kayhan International, Teheran
Kommunist, M
Krasnaya Zvezda, M
Literaturnaya Gazeta, M
Mideast Mirror, B

Miroraya Ekonomika i Mezhdunarodnye Otnosheniya, M
Mizan, L
Le Monde, Paris
An-Nahar, B
Narody Azii i Afriki, M
Neue Zurcher Zeitung, Zurich
New Middle East, L
Newsweek, NY
New Times, M
New York Times, NY
Observer, L
The Petroleum Economist, L
Petroleum Press Service, L
Pravda, M
Problems of Communism, Washington, DC
Review of International Affairs, Belgrade
Der Spiegel, Hamburg
Summary of World Broadcasts, British Broadcast Corporation, L
Sunday Telegraph, L
Sunday Times, L
Time, NY
Times, L
US News and World Report, Washington, DC
World Marxist Review (Problems of Peace and Socialism), Prague
Za Rubezhom, M

Index